UNEQUAL FRINGES
Fringe benefits
in the United Kingdom

Francis Green
George Hadjimatheou
Robin Smail

Bedford Square Press|NCVO

First published 1984 by the
Bedford Square Press of the
National Council for Voluntary Organisations
26 Bedford Square
London WC1B 3HU

ISBN 0 7199 1141 9

Printed in Great Britain by Imediaprint Limited

Series Foreword

This series of Occasional Papers was started in 1960 to supply the need for a medium of publication for studies in the field of social policy and administration which fell between the two extremes of the short article and the full-length book. Since the inception of this Series of papers, it has, however, been extended to include many which might better be described as books: comparative speed of publication being one factor that has attracted authors to us. It was thought that such a series would not only meet a need among research workers and writers concerned with contemporary social issues, but would also strengthen links between students of the subject and administrators, social workers, committee members and others with responsibilities and interest in the social services.

Contributions to the series are welcome from any source and should be submitted in the first instance to the Secretary, Social Administration Research Trust at the London School of Economics.

The series is now published by the Bedford Square Press to which all queries about this and previous titles should be addressed.

We are grateful to the Leverhulme Trust for financial support towards this project. Their help has been a highly appreciated 'fringe' benefit! The Alfred Marks Bureau has made available to us, free of charge, copies of their surveys of Fringe Benefits for Office Staff. We thank them as we also thank the ESRC Data Archive, the Department of Employment and Dr Stephen Potter from the Open University for providing us with useful statistical data. Finally we would like to thank Steve Scotland for assistance during the final stage of the project, the Secretariat at Penrhyn Road, Kingston Polytechnic for typing various drafts of this study and Janet Hussein for typing this final manuscript.

CONTENTS

page

Chapter I   ON THE IMPORTANCE OF FRINGES   1

Chapter 2   LOOKING AT THE FACTS: GROWTH AND
INEQUALITY   6
    The Growth of Fringes
    The Distribution of Fringes
    The Understimate of Inequality
    Summary
    Appendix: Further Data on Fringe Benefits

Chapter 3   ECONOMIC THEORY   40
    Introduction
    The Supply of Fringes
    The Demand for Fringes

Chapter 4   EMPIRICAL IMPLICATIONS AND PREVIOUS STUDIES   48
    Introduction
    The Main Factors
    Methodology

Chapter 5   THE DISTRIBUTION OF FRINGES: I   55
    Results from the General Household
      Survey
    Results from Townsend's Poverty
      Survey
    Summary

Chapter 6   THE DISTRIBUTION OF FRINGES: II   74
    Results from the 1978 Labour Costs
      Survey
    Summary and Conclusion: The Factors
      Explaining the Distribution of Fringes
    Appendix: Definitions and Data Sources

Chapter 7   THE GROWTH OF FRINGES   91
    Introduction
    Government Policies
    Economics and Other Factors
    Summary and Concluding Remarks
    Appendix: Some Data on Fringes and
      Changing Industrial and
      Employment Structure

Chapter 8   FRINGE BENEFIT POLICY   107
    Introduction
    The Policy Context
    Three Principles
    Taking the 'Fringe' out of some
      'Fringe Benefits'

Bibliography   123

Index   129

LIST OF TABLES

Tables

2.1   Voluntary Social Welfare Payments as a Proportion of Total Remuneration (By Industrial Sector, 1964-81).

2.2   Time-off with Pay as a Proportion of Total Remuneration (By Industrial Sector, 1964-81).

2.3   Mean Holiday Entitlements, All full-time workers (weeks).

2.4   Subsidised Services, Benefits-in-Kind, as a Proportion of Total Remuneration (By Industrial Sector, 1964-81).

2.5   All fringes, as a Proportion of Total Remuneration (By Industrial Sector, 1964-81).

2.6   Value of Total Fringe Benefits (excluding Paid Holidays) as a Proportion of Household Income, 1969.

2.7   Pension Scheme Benefits in 1969.

2.8   Pensions and Sick Pay By Income, Employees, 1976.

2.9   Pensions and Sick Pay By Social Class, Employers, 1976.

2.10 Average Employer's Pension Contributions, as a Percentage of Salary plus Bonus, Private Sector.

2.11 Value of Accruing Pension Rights due to Employers' Contributions, as a Percentage of Salary plus Bonus, Private Sector.

2.12 Value of Superannuation Benefits as a Percentage of Salary throughout Private Sector Careers on a Range Interest Assumption, 1980.

2.13 Fringe Benefit Costs Additional to Wages, (%), 1981.

2.14 Sick Pay Coverage, 1969.

2.15 Holiday By Status, 1978.

2.16 Holiday By Status for Bankers 1983: averaged days holiday.

2.17 Holidays by Income, 1980.

2.18 Allocation of Cars by Managerial Position

2.19 Company Cars by Income

2.20   Net Benefit, from Company Cars as a Proportion of Total Remuneration.

2.21   Free Group Medical Insurance Schemes: Coverage for each Employee Category, 1978 (% of Companies).

2.22   Basis on which meals were provided, 1974.

2.23   Total Fringe Benefits by job level.

2.24   Total Fringe Benefit Ratio for Top Managers.

Appendix Chapter 2

A.1   Mean Holiday Lengths for Manual and Office Workers.

A.2   Trends in Pension Benefits and Contributions in Managerial Jobs.

A.3   Holidays in different occupations, 1974-81.

A.4   Various Fringes in 1969

A.5   Average Price of Cars provided for Managers, Private Sector (£).

A.6   Private Medical Insurance Schemes for Clerical Workers, % of Firms.

A.7   Loans and Financial Assistance for House Purchase.

A.8   Loans and Financial Assistance for purposes other than House Purchase.

A.9   Proportion of Managers and Executives receiving various Fringe Benefits.

A.10 Company Shares.

5.1   G.H.S. Independent Variables

5.2   Sick Pay Entitlement.

5.3   Private Pension Entitlement.

5.4   Accommodation Linked Job.

5.5   Independent Variables.

5.6   The Probability of Entitlement to Sick Pay.

5.7   The Probability of Receiving a Pension.

5.8   The Probability of having free use of a Company Car.

5.9   Number of weeks paid holiday adjusted for earnings (HOL).

6.1   Definition of Variables.

6.2   Regression with Voluntary Social Welfare Payments as a % of wages as Dependent Variable (Series A).

6.3   Regression with Voluntary Social Welfare Payments as a % of Wages as Dependent Variable (Series B).

6.4   Regression with Benefits-in-kind as % of Wages as Dependent Variable (Series A).

6.5   Regression with Benefits-in-kind as % of Wages as Dependent Variable (Series B).

6.6   Regression with Subsidised Services as a % of Wages as Dependent Variable (Series A).

6.7   Subsidised Services - All Variables specified.

Appendix Chapter 7

A.1   Fringes by Industry, 1964-1981, and Tenure.

A.2   Labour Force Composition.

CHAPTER 1

ON THE IMPORTANCE OF FRINGES

Most economic investigations of rewards at work concentrate exclusively on wages and salaries. Since the value of other types of remuneration used to be very small it was a justifiable approximation, but in the past two decades other rewards have come to be increasingly valuable. As any high paid person knows, if one wants to know what a job is offering it is not enough to ask how much the salary is. One has to find out also about the 'fringe benefits'. These are the object of analysis of this book, for they are as yet an inadequately examined feature of the British labour market, and they have become too important to be ignored. Compared to other types of non-wage reward, for example the informal expectation of tips or illegal gains from pilfering and fiddling, fringes are normally much more valuable and can in principle be more readily amenable to empirical analysis.[1] Our examination shows that fringe benefits are received in highly unequal portions by working people.

Low paid workers in the secondary[2] sectors of the labour market are likely to receive relatively few of them. Only a small proportion belong to occupational pension schemes and these tend not to be worth very much: thus they have to rely on the state pension. Many are covered by occupational sick pay schemes which are better than the minimum statutory sick pay but by no means all, especially among those working in small firms. Some receive subsidised meals, either in a canteen or with luncheon vouchers, but this is also less likely in smaller companies. Some are entitled to buy company products at a discount, but these are not usually worth a great deal. No accurate figures are available as to how much the sum of these various benefits are worth to the average low wage worker, but it is certain that apart from holidays they amount only to a low percentage of income, of the order of perhaps six per cent.[3]

Other workers, in relatively secure jobs who tend to stay with one employer for a long period, are better off as regards fringe benefits. Most of these are members of occupational pension schemes as well as sick pay schemes, especially full-time office workers. They are more likely to receive a good package of benefits including subsidised meals, use of company sports and social facilities and so on, together with over four weeks holiday especially after a number of years service.

But their benefits are much smaller, both in absolute terms and as
a proportion of income, than those obtained by managers, executives
and others at high salary levels.   Typically a man earning an
annual salary of, say, £15,000 or above (in 1982) can in all likelihood expect to have at least five weeks paid holiday, the security
of a good sick pay scheme, an occupational pension worth perhaps 20
to 30% or even more on top of salary, a company car for private use
that could be worth up to 40% extra in terms of gross salary
equivalent,[4] and a host of other smaller benefits besides, including
expense account meals, and subscriptions for medical insurance.   A
similar calculation for the £40,000 a year private sector manager
suggests that the value of holidays, pensions and company car would
add up to between £20,000 and £25,000 a year.   Not all high paid
workers get all these benefits, but it gives some idea of their
importance that on average the sum total of fringes for managing
directors of large companies was estimated to cost firms 36% on top
of salary in 1978.   To the managers themselves they were worth more
than this since unlike salary much of that 36% gross benefit is untaxed; moreover since 1978 the figures has probably increased.[5]

Growth, Inequality and Other Issues
Fringe benefits have been received by at least some workers for a
long time, but nowadays they are more widespread.   Moreover twenty
years ago they were worth only about half what they are now in
relation to wages and salaries.   For low paid workers it was safe
largely to ignore them in economic analysis, as also did the workers
themselves in the bargaining process, excepting the question of
holidays.   Economists have not yet adequately explained why fringes
have since grown so much, and this will be one of the tasks of this
book.   It may be tempting to say that it is all due to the tax
advantages enjoyed by fringes, together with the effect of specific
exclusion clauses in governments' incomes policies, but the picture
is much more complex than that.   Some benefits, such as private
medical insurance have grown very fast in periods when they enjoyed
no tax privileges.   Others such as pensions have grown but many tax-
payers remain excluded from them for one reason or another.   And
although incomes policy exemptions may have provided a fillip to
holidays, sick pay and pensions, the fact is that these benefits have
been growing steadily for decades without their help.   These
questions are addressed in detail in Chapter 7.

Another issue, which we have already hinted at and which remains a
recurring theme throughout the book, is the persistent inequality of
treatment.   It raises two separate questions.   First, how can it
be explained?   We shall argue that, though tax exemptions play a
role, there are other important factors.   Fringe benefits can have a
divisive function both in the economy as a whole and within individual companies.   For example, the payment of occupational pension
rights to one half of the working population gives them security and
relative affluence in old age at the expense of the rest.   And within
firms, pensions can drive a wedge between sections of the work force,
by encouraging workers to be committed and loyal to the company
rather than their fellow workers.   Other fringes can also have this

effect. And company cars serve to emphasise the status differentials between management and the main workforce. Most trade unions
have traditionally been suspicious of management-initiated fringe
benefit schemes. This was not irrational since they knew they
would be used to weaken workers' allegiances to the unions.
Governments have made them pay for their suspicion: for in missing
out on fringes, as many did, they also lost out on the tax
exemptions for a long time. In the 1970s some unions began to
change tack, but the divisive act had been working then for a long
time.

Another question arising from the inequality of fringes is: given
that it exists how does this alter overall measures of inequality in
command over resources? We cannot here analyse the relevance of
all other non-wage aspects of need satisfaction, but a first step
would be to integrate fringes with money income as normally measured
in the official statistics, to give a better measure of the
inequality of total remuneration. Our investigation, discussed in
Chapter 2, shows the inequality to be greater. Even though lack of
adequate data prevents us giving a precise estimate, the approximation allows us to investigate whether observed trends in official
income inequality are meaningful pointers to changes in society's
overall inequalities.

Apart from the issue of why fringes have become such an important
aspect of the labour market, there is the associated question of how
they affect the functioning of the economy. In the first place
they considerably modify the way the labour market functions. They
increase the amount of information necessary for job-seekers to
obtain if they are to make rational choices between jobs. More
important, they inhibit mobility. Although some restrictions of
turnover can be beneficial by reducing training and other turnover
costs, many observers have argued that the limitations have been
unfair and too severe. This is particularly true of the penalties
imposed on early leavers from occupational pension schemes, but sick
pay schemes and holidays also tend to have service-related elements.

The pensions problem was originally posed by a group of progressive
managers in the 1930s[6] and was regularly noted in subsequent
decades. Recently however there has been stronger pressure on
companies and on the pension fund establishments to protect early
leavers' rights. Other labour market questions that are occasion-
ally posed concern the relationship between sick pay and absenteeism,
and between holidays and productivity.

Fringes can also have a wider effect on the economy. Well known is
the major presence of pension funds in British financial markets.
Is this beneficial for the markets and for the economy, or do they
create inefficiencies, or frustrate other government policies?
Also, there is the impact of company cars on the British motor
industry. Have they benefitted the industry by providing a large
domestic demand or harmed it by stultifying its structure? Does the

'Buy British' philosophy of company fleet managers really raise the demand for British cars or does it simply alter the structure of demand?

Finally, the growth and distribution of fringes is inevitably intertwined with the development of the welfare state. At several stages, state and company welfare strategies have interacted and modified each other. The lack of good state pensions in the 1950s and 1960s stimulated and reinforced the occupational pensions movement; but equally there was little pressure for state pension improvements while those with the power to change things could themselves expect improved occupational pensions. The combination of the two sectors came to be referred to as a 'partnership'. The National Health Service provides another case in point. Its stagnation provides the impetus for the growth of private medicine, but again the option of private preferential treatment reduces the political pressure at the top for improvements in the NHS. What these two examples show is that in discussing the policies that governments take or should take towards fringes we need always to ask how they relate to social policy in general.

The Structure of the Book

In the main part of the book we carry out a major examination of the determinants of fringe benefits in Britain - in order to see why they are paid, why they are unequally distributed and why they have grown so much in importance. We use formal statistical techniques where appropriate and possible, as well as straightforward examination of trends and of relevant facts.

Our procedure is as follows. In Chapter 2 we bring together the relevant information about fringe benefits in Britain, presenting as complete a picture as possible as to how they have grown, and how they are distributed amongst people. In Chapter 3 we develop a theory of fringes based on the literature about the structuring ('segmentation') of labour markets and on some conventional arguments concerning tax reliefs and scale economies. Chapter 4 develops the empirical implications by isolating the major economic variables which determine the payment of fringes, and looks at previous studies (mainly in the United States) to see the conclusions they draw about the importance of these factors in practice. Chapters 5 and 6 present the results of our own empirical investigations of these factors, using different data sources, concentrating on the explanation of the distribution of fringes. Chapter 7 examines a variety of explanations for the growth of fringes, and finds that quite a few factors were important. Finally, in Chapter 8 we examine the policy issues referred to above and make recommendations based on our theoretical and empirical results and on some clearly stated principles.

Footnotes

1. Working conditions, or the degree of job satisfaction, are more subjective, less easily specified and hence more difficult to examine than fringes. Informal rewards such as tips are also difficult to quantify as they are not specified in rules or contracts. Illegal gains are equally troublesome, since their recipients have an incentive to withhold honest information about them. Mars (1983) gives a sociological analysis, but little quantifiable data.

2. By 'secondary' jobs we refer to those showing some or all of the following characteristics: relatively low wages, high turnover and its concomitant short job tenure, low job security, few skills and little job satisfaction.

3. This figure is only a guess, based on an extrapolation from an estimate for the poorest fifth of the population in 1969 by Townsend (1979) but it is unlikely to be more than a few percentage points out. Note that in the Textiles industry these fringe benefits were 5.6% of wages in 1981 and this was not the lowest industry; see Table 2.13 in Chapter 2.

4. The extra money you would have to earn before tax in order to buy the car out of salary and be equally well off.

5. See Chapter 2, for details of these figures and their sources.

6. Management Research Group, 325.

CHAPTER 2

LOOKING AT THE FACTS:
GROWTH AND INEQUALITY

Introduction
Our main aim in this chapter is to examine the quantitative
importance of fringe benefits in the British economy - to build up
estimates of how much they have grown in importance and of how they
are distributed between people.

This is a necessary preliminary step since there is no alternative
single set of data to which we could refer.   This chapter, with
the appendix, brings together the information from a wide range of
data sources and provides as comprehensive a picture as it is
possible to obtain at present.   While this will hopefully be of
interest in itself to future researchers in this and related fields,
for the purposes of this book it serves to pose the context for the
questions which are addressed in our theoretical and empirical work.
For readers who do not wish to peruse too many tables, the main
conclusions are briefly summarised at the end of this chapter.

In the fourth section (after discussing growth and inequality) we
briefly pursue a corollary which is incidental to the main line of
argument in the book but which is very relevant to the question of
income distribution in general - namely, the underestimate of
inequality that derives from most fringe benefits not being counted
as part of income in the official statistics.   This lacuna is well
known but always set aside for want of adequate quantitative
information.   We cannot say precisely how much the inequality
measures are downward biased.   But it may be seen that the problem
has now become sufficiently important to render invalid and futile
the conclusions based on trends in inequality as measured from
official data.

The Growth of Fringes
It is useful to begin by precisely defining fringe benefits, since
the term is not used in entirely the same way by different people.
What is a 'perk' for some may be a 'fringe benefit' or even a 'right
at work' for others.   Moreover there are a range of job attributes
apart from the wage which could be investigated, but in this book
we concentrate only on those that are legal and whose value or cost
is easily measurable.   Thus fringes are defined to be those legal
and quantifiable benefits from work over and above earned income.
These include the following: paid holidays, sickness pay, other
time-off work with pay, occupational pension schemes, private use of

company cars, meal vouchers or subsidised meals, free or cheap goods, tied accommodation, social, medical and sports facilities, travel and removal allowances, private health insurance, cheap loans, insurance cover and payment of educational fees. Extra earned income such as overtime or bonuses are excluded from our definition of fringe benefits, as are any statutory payments such as national insurance contributions.

The most uniform and comprehensive statistical data on fringes are provided by the Department of Employment. Every few years, they carry out a Labour Cost Survey in British industry. Their results are only made available at the industry level of analysis, and they do not include the costs of providing company cars. Moreover the value to employees will for some fringes be greater than the cost incurred by employers, since they are subject to income tax exemptions. Nonetheless, their successive surveys give a reliable picture of changes in fringe benefit provision over a substantial period. It is convenient to use their categories[1] to show the growth that has occurred.

   a) Voluntary Social Welfare Payments (VSWP):
This grouping of benefits consists mainly of employers' superannuation contributions but also includes medical and life insurance. As Table 2.1 shows, these payments, as a ratio to total remuneration, nearly doubled between 1964 and 1981 for the manufacturing industries and more than doubled elsewhere with the one exception of the financial sector. It is, however, within Insurance and Banking that VSWP continue to be most significant. In 1981 they cost employers over £1,600 for the average employee, compared to less than £200 in the construction industry.

Table 2.1   Voluntary Social Welfare Payments +
               As a Proportion of Total Remuneration ++
               (By Industrial Sector, 1964-1981)

Sector	1964	1968	1973	1975	1978	1981
All Manufacturing industries	3.2	3.3	3.6	4.2	5.3	5.8
Mining and Quarrying	4.5	6.0	6.1	11.6	10.1	11.2
Construction	1.2	1.5	1.7	1.8	2.5	3.1
Gas, Electricity and Water	6.6	6.6	8.3	9.1	13.2	14.4
Transport and Communication	6.2	6.2	-	-	-	-
Insurance and Banking	16.5	13.3	-	16.5[1]	16.6[2]	16.2
Non-Industrial Civil Service and Local Authorities	6.0	6.2	-	-	-	-
Distributive Trades	-	-	-	3.1[1]	4.7	5.2

1   = for 1974
2   = Insurance, Banking and Other Financial Institutions
+   = Superannuation and pension funds, provision for sickness and
      industrial accidents, lump sum, ex gratia and other voluntary
      payments
++ = Total fringes plus wages and salaries

The rising importance of VSWP is not due to increasing proportions of the workforce becoming members of pension schemes. The numbers grew from 2.6 million in 1936 to 11.1 million by 1963, but thereafter did not change very substantially - the latest figure is 11.8 million in 1979. Rather, the increase in pension costs is attributable to rises in contribution and benefit levels. Thus, as a proportion of disposable income, contributions by both employees and employers have risen steadily from under 4% in 1953 to 8.4% in 1981.[2] As a result pension rights have become a significant part of the income and wealth of households, while the funds which guarantee many of these rights have become important influences on the capital market. At a £110 billion, they accounted for 11% of household wealth in 1890.[3] Moreover, employees' contributions, employers' contributions, investment income to funds and capital gains on funds are all tax-free, probably representing tax avoidance of over £5 billion each year.[4]

Also included under VSWP is private medical insurance. This has been a particularly fast growing fringe since about 1978 for executives and also for office staff. (Appendix, Tables A6 and A9). Total subscribers grew rapidly until 1982, by which time there were over 1.9 million subscribers (72% of which were through company group schemes) covering over 4.2 million insured people. Since then the growth has slowed somewhat. Another element of VSWP is the cost of payments into sickness funds, the bulk of money for sickness is accounted as pay for time off work, which we now examine.

b) <u>Holidays and Other Time Off with Pay</u>:
Altogether sickness costs amounted to some 1.7% of wages and salaries in 1981. In 1961 only 57% of full-time workers were covered by sick pay schemes - the rest had to rely on meagre National Insurance benefits. The proportions rose to 73% in 1970 and 79% in 1974, but we have no information whether the numbers expanded yet more in recent years, or whether they reached a plateau. Most part-time workers continued without any (private) cover for sickness. From April 1983, however, the government has compelled employers to provide cover for short-term sickness - called 'Statutory Sick Pay' - for all workers. But the major element in Table 2.2 is paid holiday leave. The rise in this element of remuneration reflects steady improvements brought about over a long period of time. At the turn of the century few people (mainly non-manual) were entitled to paid holidays. By the end of the 1940s most manual workers had gained the right to a week's leave apart from public holidays, (while non-manuals had more); by 1960 this had risen to two weeks. Table 2.3 shows the improvements since then. By the 1980s most manual workers, as well as clerical workers, had reached four weeks (see Appendix, Table A1).

Table 2.2   Time-Off With Pay ≠
                   As A Proportion of Total Remuneration
                      (By Industrial Sector, 1964-1981)

| | | | | Year | | |
Sector	1964	1968	1973	1975	1978	1981
All Manufacturing industries	6.3	7.6	9.5	10.0	10.1	11.2
Mining and Quarrying	8.1	9.0	13.4	11.5	10.0	9.6
Construction	4.8	5.7	0.2	7.7	7.5	8.7
Gas, Electricity and Water	9.7	11.0	11.9	11.9	12.1	12.6
Transport and Communication	8.1	10.4	-	-	-	-
Insurance and Banking	8.1	9.9	-	-	-	-
Non-Industrial Civil Service						
and Local Authorities	11.0	11.6	-	-	-	-
Distributive Trades	-	-	-	-	-	-

≠ = For holidays, sickness or other time off with pay.
   Source:

In absolute terms, time off with pay costs for example some £500 in
1981 in the construction industry.

Table 2.3   Mean Holiday Entitlements,
                   All Full-Time Workers (Weeks)

	Males	Females
1968	2.45	2.54
1974	3.68	3.20
1981	4.60	4.60

Source: New Earnings Surveys.

    c) Subsidised Services and Benefits in Kind:
Subsidised services include subsidies on staff canteens, medical and
health services, recreational, cultural and educational services,
transport to and from work, the provision of work clothes, removal of
household effects and assistance with housing.   'Benefits in Kind'
refers to meal vouchers and the provision of free or cheap goods.
As Table 2.4 shows, this grouping is less significant than the
previous two, and has also tended to grow by a lesser amount.   However for the average worker in either Insurance and Banking or Mining
and Quarrying, the cost of these benefits was particularly high in
absolute terms, amounting to about £800 in 1981.

Since the provision of free or cheap goods amounted fairly steadily to
just over 0.1 per cent of remuneration for most years reported, most
growth arose from increases in the other benefits.

9

Table 2.4   Subsidised Services, Benefits-in-Kind
             As A Proportion of Total Remuneration
             (By Industrial Sector, 1964-1981)

Sector	Year					
	1964	1968	1973	1975	1978	1981
All Manufacturing industries	1.6	2.4	2.0	1.9	2.3	2.3
Mining and Quarrying	7.2	7.2	7.0	6.6	7.7	7.6
Construction	1.7	2.4	2.0	1.8	2.1	2.0
Gas, Electricity and Water	1.4	2.3	2.3	2.2	2.4	2.4
Transport and Communication	2.0	2.2	-	-	-	-
Insurance and Banking	1.6	5.2	-	6.7[1,2]	6.7	8.6
Non-Industrial Civil Service and Local Authorities	1.4	2.3	-	-	-	-
Distributive Trades	-	-	-	3.1[1]	2.2	1.9

1 = 1974
2 = Insurance, Banking and Other Financial Institutions.

d) All Fringes:

Table 2.5 shows the results of adding up where possible the costs of
all the fringes so far mentioned.   They rose nearly twice as fast
as wages and salaries between 1964 and 1981, and by the end of the
period accounted for nearly 20 per cent of remuneration in manufacturing and more elsewhere.   In Insurance and Banking they had come
to cost over £3,400 annually per employee.   Yet these figures do
not fully capture the value of fringe benefits to workers.   This is
partly because they are in many cases exempt from tax, so that to
the tax-paying employee fringes are worth more, pound for pound,
than the same amount in payroll costs.   But also, a major fringe is
omitted from the figures: company cars.   Curiously, the provision
of cars for private use is not regarded as a labour cost for the
purposes of the Department of Employment's surveys!

Table 2.5   All Fringes
             As A Proportion of Total Remuneration
             (By Industrial Sector, 1964-1981)

Sector	Year					
	1964	1968	1973	1975	1978	1981
All Manufacturing industries	11.1	13.3	15.1	16.1	17.7	19.4
Mining and Quarrying	19.9	22.2	26.6	29.6	27.8	28.5
Construction	7.7	9.6	10.8	11.3	12.0	13.8
Gas, Electricity and Water	17.7	19.9	22.5	23.2	27.6	29.4
Transport and Communication	16.3	18.8	-	-	-	-
Insurance and Banking	26.2	28.4	-	-	-	-
Non-Industrial Civil Service and Local Authorities	18.4	20.1	-	-	-	-

The growth rates are impressive.   In 1970 a half of all managers
and executives had full use of a company car.   By 1983 the figure
was 77 per cent (while a further 7% had a car allowance);
(Appendix, Table A9).   The proportion of new cars bought by companies rose from about 20-25% in 1965 to around 50-60% in 1983.[5]
By then, the tax relief on the capital and running costs of company
cars was at least £730 million and possibly as much as £2.3 billion
annually.[6]

The Distribution of Fringes
If the value of fringe benefits is added to wages and salaries to
give total remuneration, the resulting inequality between households
is greater than if we confine attention only to incomes.   Rich
people do not simply receive more fringes than the poor: they get
more in relation to already high incomes.

The evidence for this begins with Table 2.6, which shows the highly
unequal fringes prevailing in 1969.   Thus measures of income inequality are under-estimates of true inequality at that time.

Table 2.6   Value of Total Fringe Benefits
                        (Excluding Paid Holidays)
                As Proportion of Household Income, In 1969

Quintiles of Household Income	% of Income
Top 20%	13.3
Second 20%	11.4
Third 20%	8.9
Fourth 20%	6.9
Bottom 20%	2.6

Source: Calculated from Townsend (1979), p.229, with correction for
          printing error.

Has this underestimate increased or decreased in importance over the
1970s till the present?   On the one hand the overall level of
fringes has become steadily more substantial, and if these are distributed in the same way as in 1969 current measures of income inequality must be increasingly unreliable.   On the other hand, there
may have been some catching up by the poorer quintiles, as certain
fringes became more widely available.

Government sources of statistics do not provide us with adequate
data on fringe values at each income level.   But we are able to
draw on a variety of sources to build up a picture for each major
fringe.

     a) Occupational Pensions
        Coverage:
Secondary analysis of Townsend's unique survey shows that much of
the inequality of fringes in 1969 arose from occupational pensions,

11

whose value was greatest for the richer quintiles.   Table 2.7 indicates how these benefits were dispersed:

Table 2.7   Pension Scheme Benefits in 1969

Quintiles of Household Income	Proportion of employees ⧸ expecting a pension from their employer on retirement	Proportion of employees⧸ expecting a lump sum on their retirement
	%	%
Top 20%	46	16
Second 20%	44	15
Third 20%	40	11
Fourth 20%	31	9
Bottom 20%	13	4

⧸ All numbers are probably underestimates of actual (as opposed to perceived) membership of pension schemes.   In each case there were a number of no replies or 'don't knows'.   If the lower paid were less aware of pension benefits, these figures may overstate the actual dispersion.

Since then, the total numbers in schemes has stayed roughly constant, while the contributions and benefits have steadily increased.   This suggests that, if anything, occupational pension benefits are nowadays even more unequally distributed across the whole population. But this must be balanced by the improvements in state pension rights for the remaining half of the workforce.   The overall trend in (state plus occupation) pensions inequality cannot therefore be easily judged.[7]   Nonetheless it is useful to look for any changes in the distribution of occupational pension rights.   Has there been any degree of equalisation within this sector?

Table 2.8 shows that in 1976 pension scheme membership remained unequal, with those on higher incomes more likely to belong.   This inequality is mirrored by differences between various occupations as shown in Table 2.9.

There may have been some movement towards equalisation of coverage between manual and non-manual workers, reflecting the philosophy that many job status distinctions between clerical and factory workers had become artificial and outdated.   Personnel management guides propounded change, and the mood seemed to be to establish single status for all workers in many companies (Murlis and Grist, 1976).   In total, 45% of scheme members were manual workers in 1975, compared to 42% in 1971: not much of a change.   Unfortunately, the 1979 Government Actuary survey did not publish the proportions of manual workers.   However, over and above differences in membership rates, schemes for manual workers have traditionally been separate from and less valuable than those for non-manuals.   Some of these differences were eroded in the 1970s, to the extent that by 1983 according to the British Institute of Management, 80% of companies had the same scheme for all employees regardless of status.

Value:

The only information about the value of occupational pensions shows that this probably increased over the decade for private sector high paid managers, and is now very substantial in proportion to salary. Most managers look forward to a pension of some two thirds of final pay, plus substantial other benefits.

Table 2.8   Pensions and Sick Pay By Income,
                        Employees, 1976

Income Band	Proportion in Occupational Pension Schemes	Proportion who get paid when sick
	%	%
Under £500	22.1	44.0
£500 - £1000	8.9	47.5
£1000 - £1500	19.4	63.8
£1500 - £2000	38.1	72.6
£2000 - £2500	56.4	74.8
£2500 - £3000	63.9	74.5
£3000 - £3500	71.6	76.1
£3500 - £4500	77.6	82.7
£4500 - £5000	88.6	89.8
£5000 - £6000	82.7	91.6
£6000 - £7000	85.2	94.3
Over £7000	89.4	97.6

Source: Secondary analysis of General Household Survey, 1976

Table 2.9   Pensions and Sick Pay By Social Class,
                        Employees, 1976

	Proportion in Occupational Pension Schemes	Proportion who get paid when sick
	%	%
Professionals	74.8	92.4
Employers and Managers	67.7	91.1
Intermediate and Junior Managers	48.8	79.0
Skilled Manual	50.7	57.2
Semi-Skilled Manual	34.2	53.8
Unskilled Manual	22.5	50.4

Source: Secondary analysis of General Household Survey, 1976

Table 2.10 shows large increases in employers' contributions to pension schemes for the rich, from 1973 to 1977. Independent confirmation of this trend is shown by the rise in employers' pension contributions, and in various pension benefits, for managers generally, over 1970 to 1978; (Appendix , Table A2). A further survey in 1980 suggests high contribution levels were broadly maintained, but no direct comparison is possible due to a change in definitions.

Table 2.10 <u>Average Employer's Pension Contribution As</u>
<u>Percentage of Salary Plus Bonus</u>,
<u>Private Sector</u>

	1973	1977
Chairman	16.2	26.9
Deputy Chairman	17.4	27.0
Main Board Members	17.5	22.9
Senior Executives	15.2	20.4

Source: Review Body on Top Salaries, Chairman Lord Boyle:
          REPORT ON TOP SALARIES, Appendix 4, Cmnd. 5846 and
          SECOND REPORT, Appendix E, Cmnd. 7253.

Table 2.11 shows changes in the value of accruing pension rights, as a proportion of money income, estimated by the Government Actuary: the increase here is not so marked. In 1980, new calculations shown in Table 2.12 were made using a range of interest rate assumptions. Although the values are uncertain, it is plain that they are very substantial. To take one example, the chief executive's pension in a financial company is typically worth <u>at least</u> 30% on top of salary.

Table 2.11 <u>Value of Accruing Pension Rights Due To</u>
<u>Employers Contributions, As Percentage Of</u>
<u>Salary Plus Bonus, Private Sector</u>

	1973	1977
Main Board Members	18.6	20.7
Senior Executives	15.9	15.8

Source: As for Table 2.10.

There can be little doubt that average and lower paid workers' pensions are not worth anything like these amounts. Moreover there are millions of workers who do not belong to an occupational pension scheme, while those who are unemployed are not even contributing to the state scheme. Pension benefits remain very unequal. We do not know enough to allocate the rising values to various income groups but it is clear that the higher paid were not excluded.

Table 2.12   Value Of Superannuation Benefits
As A Percentage of Salary Throughout
Private Sector Careers On A Range
Of Interest Assumptions, 1980

Per cent of salary

| Sector | Chief executive | Other Main Board member[a] | Senior executive | |
			Level 1	Level 2
Non-financial Turnover (£ million)				
800 and over	38-60	30-50	24-42	24-42
400 but under 800	31-49	28-46	23-39	21-38
200 but under 400	30-51	26-44	20-36	
100 but under 200	26-43	23-35	18-32	b
50 but under 100	22-37	18-32	14-26	
25 but under 50	17-28	15-27	13-23	
Financial	30-49	c	24-42	23-40

a   Excluding deputy chief executives
b   Survey information not collected
c   Insufficient information
Source: Review Body of Top Salaries, 1982, Chairman Lord Plowden:
          FIFTH REPORT ON TOP SALARIES, Appendix F. Cmnd. 8552.

Since different kinds of workers are to be found in varying proportions between industries, the inequalities we have enumerated are,
not surprisingly, reflected in differences in average pension coverage and costs between industries.   Table 2.13 shows that costs
ranged betweekn 2% and 19% of wages and salaries in 1981.   Construction, clothing, leather and textiles industries have relatively
low values, while chemicals and coal and petroleum, mining and
energy industries have especially high coverage.   These differences,
which may be observed for previous years also, confirm once again the
extra inequalities amongst persons attributable to pensions.

Table 2.13   Fringe Benefit Costs Additional
                To Wages, (%), 1981

Industry Group	Occupational Pensions	Sick Pay≁	Holidays & Other Time Off With Pay	Benefits In Kind	Subsidised Services
All Manufacturing	6.8	1.71	12.19	0.16	1.78
All Index of Production Industries	7.42	1.70	11.90	0.39	1.80
Food, drink & Tobacco	7.47	2.24	11.56	0.38	2.72
Coal & Petroleum Products	16.19	2.45	11.07	1.44	3.76
Chemicals & Allied Industries	12.05	2.84	12.23	0.12	3.11
Metal Manufacture	8.42	0.85	11.41	0.26	1.18
Mechanical Engineering	6.44	1.59	12.44	0.11	1.64
Instrument Engineering	7.53	2.38	12.85	0.08	1.86
Electrical Engineering	5.62	2.07	12.67	0.07	1.77
Ship Building & Marine Engineering	5.57	1.84	11.77	0.07	1.40
Vehicles	7.97	2.42	14.15	0.11	2.05
Metal Goods not elsewhere specified	5.37	1.11	12.34	0.15	1.25
Textiles	3.44	0.93	11.45	0.11	1.11
Leather, Leathergoods and Fur	2.80	0.31	10.42	0.06	1.26
Clothing and Footwear	2.25	0.43	11.64	0.11	1.07
Bricks, Pottery, Glass, Cement etc.	5.97	1.17	11.76	0.16	1.57
Timber, Furniture etc.	3.78	0.82	10.51	0.09	0.90
Paper, Printing and Publishing	6.50	1.49	11.70	0.12	1.19
Other Manufacturing	5.88	1.31	11.92	0.13	1.64
Mining & Quarrying	14.69	1.83	11.95	4.71	4.04
Construction	3.40	0.80	9.51	0.10	1.03
Gas, Electicity and Water	19.27	3.68	14.31	0.09	1.96

≁ Cost of sick pay plus payments into schemes for sickness and
   industrial accidents.   Other definitions, see Tables 1 and 2.
Source: Department of Employment, unpublished tables.

   b) Sick Pay

Coverage:
Table 2.14 shows that entitlement to sick pay was also unequally
distributed in 1969.   As Tables 2.8 and 2.9 indicate, this inequality remained in 1976: those in higher income brackets were more
likely to be covered by a sick pay scheme, as were those in non-
manual as opposed to manual occupations.

Table 2.14   Sick Pay Coverage in 1969

Quintile	Proportion of employees who would get paid when sick
Top 20%	61
Second 20%	54
Third 20%	47
Fourth 20%	42
Bottom 20%	23

During the 1970s there was probably some degree of catching up by manual workers. For some groups of non-manual workers coverage was almost universal by the beginning of the decade, so the overall improvement that occurred must have involved some equalisation. A comparison of extremes across industries illustrates this point: from 1970 to 1974 the proportion of workers covered in the metal manufacture industry rose from 31% to 68%, whereas in the coal and petroleum industry it went from 94% to 97%.[8] Two British Institute of Management Surveys, Murlis and Grist (1976) and Murlis (1978) also suggest the same point, even though the two are not strictly comparable. The former found that 40% of companies had no sick pay schemes for manual workers, while in the latter the figure was 32%.

But even though the proportions of manual workers covered by schemes improved, their quality remains at present generally below those for non-manuals and managers. On average the 'waiting days' (before sick pay begins) are more, the qualifying period (months spent with the company) is longer, the level of sick pay a lower proportion of normal pay and the period of entitlement shorter, for manual workers.[9]

    Value:
The differences in coverage and in quality are in turn reflected in variations of labour costs in industries, (though these will also be affected by variations in sickness rates). In 1981, sickness and industrial accident payments amounted on average to nearly 2% of pay for non-manual workers in all the Production Industries, compared to just over 1½% for manuals. And, as Table 2.13 shows, sick pay costs ranged across industries from only 0.31% in Leather and Fur to 3.68% in Gas, Electricity and Water.

As with pensions, estimating the overall impact on inequality of sick pay is complicated by the co-existence of private sick pay schemes alongside state sickness benefits which are also changing. In 1983 the private and public support systems were merged for short term spells of sickness: employers are now obliged to pay Statutory Sick Pay (SSP) to ill employees, for which they are compensated by reduced National Insurance Contributions. The majority of workers were previously in 'inclusive' schemes, whereby the amount paid out included a deduction for the benefit that could be claimed from the state. These were probably little affected by the change to the new system.

A smaller proportion (in 1975 11% of men and 22% of women) used to get state sickness benefit on top of sick pay, which could often mean they were financially better off being ill than fit. These will have lost out under the new Statutory Sick Pay system. Finally those workers who previously had to rely on state benefits when sick will on average be worse off under the new system, since the level of SSP is set so low; but this varies from person to person according to how many dependents he or she had, because this previously affected the level of state benefits.

c) Paid Holidays
Coverage:
Higher paid and higher status workers tend to have longer paid holidays, but the right to some paid leave is universal among regular full time workers.

Table 2.15 illustrates the degree of inequality in 1978. For example, 64% of companies gave directors over 4 weeks holiday compared to only 5% for manual workers. A survey of bankers in 1983, Table 2.16, suggests that status differentials remain, especially as far as basic entitlement is concerned.

Table 2.15   Holidays by Status, 1978

Status	Proportion of companies giving basic entitlement of more than 20 days (%)
Directors	64
Senior Managers	55
Middle Managers	40
Junior Managers	29
Clerical	9
Manual	5

Source: H. Murlis (1978)

Table 2.16   Holidays by Status for Bankers, 1983

	average days holidays/	
	Non Officers	Most senior employees
Basic entitlement	20.0	25.3
Maximum entitlement	24.0	26.2

Source: J. Wren & Co. (1983)
/ unweighted average of 41 banks.

Meanwhile Table 2.17 confirms that better holidays are normally given with jobs at higher income levels.

All this evidence applies to full time workers. Part timers are likely to have on average much less paid holiday and indeed many part timers, along with agency temps and others in casual labour markets, have none at all. And of course the unemployed also receive no hol-paid holidays. All these certainly decrease the amounts of this benefit going to lower income households but lack of data do not allow us to quantify the effects.

Table 2.17   Holidays by Income, 1980

Jobs with a maximum annual salary of: (£)	After 1 year's service	After 10 years service
Up to 4999	19.5	22.5
5000 to 6999	21.0	24.2
7000 to 8999	21.7	24.6
9000 to 10,999	21.8	24.5
11,000 to 12,999	22.6	25.2
Over 13,000	23.2	25.4

Source: Calculated from Table 6, Appendix 10, Report of Civil Service Pay Research Unit Board, 1980.

However, while the differences in holidays between the lower and higher paid are clear, they are not so great and so blatant as with some other fringes, such as pensions and company cars (see below). Over the past decade, there has been some catching up by manual workers (who are, on average, lower paid). The growth in annual holidays for manuals was considerable, and exceeded that for non-manuals: on average, manual workers were about 23% worse off than non-manuals in 1974, but by 1981 this had been reduced to 13%; (Tables A1 and A3 in the Appendix show how different occupations fared). Across industries, this is reflected in the fact that holi-day costs as a proportion of wages lie between 10 and 13% in most cases (see Table 2.13) which is not a very wide range.

d) Company Cars
Coverage:
In 1969 company cars were unequally distributed across income groups (see Appendix, Table A4), but they were not then a very important part of remuneration. For the richest 20% of the population they amounted to perhaps 1% of income. Since then however they have grown steadily in importance as a way of paying high income earners, particularly executives and managers in the private sector. As a result they now have a substantial impact on the distribution of in-come.

By now, most executives and almost all directors receive this benefit (Appendix, Table A9). Table 2.18 indicates the way cars were allocated in 1982 according to job levels. In most cases cars are provided on grounds of status alone, though of course for several middle level management posts, such as salesmen, a car is a necessary part of the job. Manual workers almost never have the private use of a company car.

Table 2.18 Allocation of Cars by Managerial Position

(% of companies)

Managing Director/ Chief Executive	95
Senior Managers	93
Middle Managers	63
Junior Managers	27
Salesforce	79
Service Engineers	30

Source: Woodmansey, 1982

Tables 2.19(a) and 2.19(b) show how those on higher incomes are much more likely to have a company car than the low paid.

Value:

Not only have the proportions of the higher paid receiving company cars substantially grown, the average benefit from cars provided has almost certainly risen faster than salaries.

Table 2.19 Company Cars by Income

Household Income (£)	(a) Proportion of House holds with Company Purchased Car (%)	(b) Jobs with a maximum salary of: (£)	Proportion of jobs with Company cars provided(%)
Under 2000	0	8000 - 9999	12.3
2000 - 3000	4	10,000 - 11,999	24.5
3000 - 4000	5	12,000 - 13,999	41.4
4000 - 5000	6	14,000 - 15,999	68.3
5000 - 6000	8	16,000 - 17,999	68.0
6000 - 7500	9	18,000 - 19,999	90.7
7500 - 10,000	10	Over 20,000	94.6
Over 10,000	13		

Source: Potter and Cousins (1983) Source: Report of the Civil Service Pay Research Unit Board, Appendix 10, 1980.

From 1973 to 1980 the prices paid for new company cars rose by a factor of between 3 and 4, while managerial salaries less than doubled (see Table A5 in Appendix).   Estimates of the benefit to employees depend on assumptions being made about capital and running costs, and, more importantly, about what proportions of total car usage is for private purposes.   Table 2.20 shows some estimates made by the Review Body on Top Salaries,[10] assuming a 50:50 split between business and private use.

Table 2.20   Net Benefit/ from Company Cars
                    As Proportion of Total Remuneration, %

	Main Board Members	Senior Executives
1973	4.0	3.1
1977	4.7	5.0

/ Capital and running costs minus employee contributions
Source: see Text

Much of the increase between the two years was due to employees being required to make lower contributions.   Further estimates of
benefits made in 1975 for the Royal Commission on the Distribution
of Income and Wealth (Report No.3) for a top manager earning nearly
£16,000 p.a. salary, ranged from 4% to nearly 12% of salary on the
basis of one third and 100% private usage assumptions respectively.
Because of the enormous tax advantages enjoyed by company car users,
these were equivalent to between 7% and 23% on top of gross salary.

Our own estimates for 1982 suggest that these benefits are of late
yet greater.   For example, the average general manager had an
annual salary of £24,240, while his car was probably worth over
£10,000 per annum, gross salary equivalent, an extra 40%.   This
would mean that the effective tax rate on the car was about 7% or
less.   Meanwhile, for the personnel executive full use of a company
car was worth about £4,500 gross salary equivalent, 27% of the
average salary for this grade.[11,12]

In view of the enormous tax advantages on company cars, it is likely
that in 1978/79, when marginal income tax rates reached 83 per cent,
the value of this fringe to high earners was even greater.   Set
against the reduction of marginal tax rates since then however, is
the increased usage of company cars.   On balance, therefore, it is
hard to assess the recent shifts in the effective income distribution
caused by company cars.   But whatever uncertainties surround the
valuation of company car benefits, it is fairly clear that throughout the 1970s they added to the inequality of income in the UK and
that in future they will continue to do so unless far reaching
measures are taken to curb their value.   Company cars must no longer
be ignored in the assessment of income distribution.

        e) Private Medical Insurance
Coverage:
A survey of top employees in June 1983 found that, out of 43 banks,
41 provided free medical insurance (mainly through BUPA) while the
other two provided it heavily subsidised.   In 32 banks, the
employees' dependents were also covered.

Such benefits have only recently been so widely available for the
higher paid.   Free insurance was given to only 1/6 of managers and
senior executives in 1970, but by 1982 nearly 2/3 could expect it
(Appendix, Table A9), and many others obtained discounts.   Table

2.21 shows that free coverage was more likely for the higher status
employees in 1978.   Since then medical insurance has spread particularly among office staff: by 1983 some 32% of companies gave free
cover, and another 41% subsidised private health coverage; (see
Appendix, Table A6).   Even a minute proportion of manual workers
have now negotiated this benefit, in spite of opposition from the
trade union movement.

Table 2.21   Free Group Medical Insurance Schemes:
               Coverage for Each Employee Category,
                    1978 (% of Companies)

Directors	74
Senior Managers	63
Middle Managers	38
Junior Managers	13
Clerical Workers	3

NB: In 11% of companies, schemes covered all employees.   These
     were all small companies, with very few manual workers.
Source: Murlis (1978)

Value:

Medical insurance may be valued by the average annual premium cost
per employee: about £130 for members of the Main Board, and £100
for Senior Executives in private companies in 1980, or, roughly 0.5%
of salary plus bonus.[13]   Where schemes are available for monthly or
weekly paid staff they are typically worth less since they require
greater contribution from the employees.

Thus private medical insurance is very unequally distributed, even
though it is now more widely available for office workers.   Its
growth undoubtedly has an effect on (and is affected by) the decline
of the National Health Service.   But the value of the benefits
probably has only a small direct effect on the distribution of
income.

     f)   Meal Benefits

These are provided in various ways to employees.   Manual workers
typically use a works canteen, while non-manuals are often provided
with separate facilities.   Directors sometimes also have their own
separate facilities.   Luncheon vouchers are often provided for
workers in the London area.   Do these different forms result in
relatively unequal benefits?

Table 2.22 shows some degree of inequality of treatment in 1974.
Top and middle management were most likely to get free meals.   However most workers gained some sort of benefit, and although the high
paid director or executive was liable to eat in better style than the
average worker, we cannot be sure whether the average benefit, as a
proportion of salary, was also higher.

Table 2.22 Basis on Which Meals were Provided, 1974

	Top Management	Middle Management	Junior Management	Clerical	Manual
At cost	8	8	8	8	8
Partially subsidised	72	80	84	85	87
Free	20	12	8	7	5

Source: Murlis (1974)

In 1969 the ratio of meal benefits to income was roughly the same for all income groups (see Appendix, Table A4).   The proportions of managers and executives receiving subsidised meals has risen only slightly, from 67% in 1970 to 71% in 1982.   The proportions of office staff receiving benefits remained much the same, and there has been no major trend to bring manual workers in line with clerical staff.   Meal benefits for the highly paid were estimated in 1980 to be 1.7% of salary plus bonus for senior executives, and 1.4% for Members of Main Boards.[14]   With the tax advantages gained these were worth yet more in terms of equivalent gross salary.   But without further data we cannot determine the relative advantages for low and high-paid workers.

g) Company Loans for House Purchase and Other Purposes
Coverage:
House purchase loans, when available, are generally fairly open to all types of employees.   But they are confined largely to the financial sector where the proportion of manual workers is relatively small.   Other loans are spread more widely among differing sectors of the economy.   Those for car purchase are predominantly a management benefit, but others such as season ticket loans are somewhat more equally available to all employee groups.

Value:
The amounts borrowed are normally related to income, so managers and executives benefit most in absolute terms.   In the mid 1970s the implied amount of subsidy could be substantial, between about 6% and 10% in terms of gross salary equivalent for those top managers receiving house loans.   Other loans yielded a similar benefit, though this came to be less important by 1980.   However since at most 13% and usually rather less of this group actually took up each type of loan, the overall effect on income distribution is not very great. (Appendix, Tables A7 and A8).

h) Life Assurance
Some companies provide free or subsidised life assurance schemes, apart from pension arrangements.   Such benefits are quite unequally distributed.   In 1969 4% of employees in the richest quintile received it, but nobody in the poorest group did (Appendix, Table A4). There is however not much data on the recent distribution of life

assurance. The proportions of managers receiving it, either
separately or through their pension schemes rose from 75% in 1974 to
92% in 1982 (Appendix, Table A9). What is more, the amounts
insured have increased since 1979 so that nearly 40% had, in 1983,
life assurance cover of over 3 times their salary. And where cover
is provided, in just under a half of companies there are separate
rules of calculation for each grade; (Murlis, 1978). A common
rule, for example, is that Executives and Qualified Technicians get
2 times salary, Foremen and Supervisiors 1½ times salary, while
Clerical, Secretarial and Manual grades get only a half of salary.

It is impossible to quantify the annual worth of many life assurance
benefits as their cost is often included in with pension schemes.
We can however be fairly confident that the extent and value of
coverage remains unequal.

    i) Company Shares
Also unequal is the possibility of buying company shares at below
market prices. About 1 in 5 top managers used to receive this
benefit and for some it could be worth anything up to about 7% above
salary plus bonus. However, for most they were worth less than
this, and the benefits by 1980 became less common and less valuable.
(Appendix, Table A.10). Recently this benefit appears to be growing again through the use of 'approved deferred share trust' schemes:
according to Inbucon (1983) over 30% were receiving the benefit of
share option or purchase schemes by 1983. We do not however have
any estimates of how much these are now worth, and hence as to how
much impact they have on distribution.

    j) Benefits in Kind
Free or cheap goods are provided by quite a few companies - in 1978,
just under half - but in most cases they are offered to all
employees. Typically, the benefit given is the company's own
products: miners get free coal, tyre makers cheap tyres, and so on.
As Table 2.13 shows, those in the Mining and Quarrying and Coal and
Petroleum Products industries do especially well. Evidence for
1969 suggests a fairly even distribution of coverage of these benefits across income groups, except that the poorest quintile was
rather worse off. (Appendix, Table A4). But their value has been
and still is greater for non-manual than for manual workers. As a
proportion of wages or salaries, they amount on average to just over
0.2% for non-manuals, twice that for manuals.

Although unequal, these benefits are not large enough to substantially affect the income distribution.

    k) Assistance with Children's Education
A small fraction of employees are given funds to pay for their children's private education. In 1977, for example, an estimated 1.7% of
senior executives received an average of £787, just under 6% of their
average salary.[15] For those top paid managers who get them, the advantages are considerable.

However their provision is limited to a small and probably diminishing number, and the overall effect on income distribution is not significant.

1) Other Miscellaneous Benefits

All other benefits have very little impact on an individual's remuneration. Moreover, while some are quite widespread - for example, sports facilities - they are usually available for all types of employee. We do not need to consider their impact on inequality.

The Underestimate of Inequality

A major criticism of official income distribution statistics is that they leave out of account those fringe benefits which are not taxed, and a portion of the true value of some which are.[16] Here, we use the information collected in the last section to assess the magnitude of the problem. We find that it shouldnot be ignored.

Official estimates are based on Inland Revenue data, supplemented by the Family Expenditure Survey and the New Earnings Survey. Neither of these surveys collect information on fringes - with the insignificant exception of income in kind for agricultural and domestic workers. Of course, there are other deficiencies in the data, or problems with the interpretation, such as the effects of changing family and age compositions of the population, the neglect of capital gains and of the black economy, and so on. But the exclusion of fringes is an increasingly important and remediable gap. It would be relatively simple to gain useful information, in the context of existing surveys, which would assist both in assessing trends in income distribution and in estimating the effects of future policy (for example, in the calculation of lost tax revenue). As it is, the General Household Survey unaccountably stopped collecting qualitative information on pension and sick pay schemes in 1976.

An order-of-magnitude hypothetical example shows that any observed trends in income distribution are dwarfed by the sort of correction that would be needed to account for fringes. We used Atkinson's inequality statistic,[17] to calculate the inequality across quintile income groups. Adding Townsend's estimates of fringe values excluding holidays (Table 2.6) to the official data,[18] the inequality measure for 1969/70 is raised from 8.16% to 8.93%. In the period to 1978/79 aggregate fringes excluding holidays had risen at least 1½ times as fast as money income. Making the assumption that fringes were distributed then in the same way as in 1969, the 1978/79 inequality measure would be raised from 8.02% to 9.22%. Thus the upward adjustment to the inequality measure, were fringes to be included, would be much greater than the stated trend in money income inequality over the decade. Indeed there would, under these assumptions, have been a notable rise in inequality - not a slight fall.

In fact it seems likely that the assumption made was, if anything, too conservative. Most of the fringes not included in the official

statistics have become yet more unequally distributed than before.
The main ones left out of account are: employers' and employees'
pension contributuions, a large proportion of the private benefit
from company cars, holidays, approved sick pay insurance, subsidised
canteens, approved life assurance, luncheon vouchers up to 15p a
working day, subsidised mortgages, share option schemes and low
value personal loans.   Of these, the first four are quantitatively
the most significant.

Occupational pensions have grown and remain very unequal with no
evidence of any catching up by the lower paid.   Company cars have
unquestionably grown more unequal over the years.   Paid holidays
are effectively days of free leisure time.   Increasing them is
normally an alternative to raising wages, and as such represents a
way of raising rewards without raising taxes.   Moreover, unequal
holiday entitlements do not show up in the income statistics.
Again, therefore, income inequality is downward biased.   But in
this case, although all holidays have increased for full-timers
manual workers have caught up somewhat.   We cannot therefore say
how the underestimate has changed over the years, but in any case
this benefit is much more equally distributed than either pensions
or company cars.   Lesser benefit are sick pay schemes, which are
fairly widespread but remain more beneficial on the whole for higher
paid workers, despite the trend in the 1970s towards harmonisation
of policies.   Of the remaining benefits some such as share option
schemes, are decidedly unequal, but they are not sufficiently widespread and valuable to have a major impact on distribution.

What do these various observations add up to?   They suggest that,
as fringes become a greater part of remuneration, and as the untaxed
and unrecorded part of remuneration is increasing, the extent of
bias in official estimates of income inequality is large and
increasing.

This conclusion is based on examining each fringe benefit separately.
We cannot confirm it by accurately allocating fringes to income
groups in recent years, in the manner of Table   2.6 for 1969.   But
existing figures do provide some confirmation.   Table 2.23 gives
estimates of fringe values (including holidays) at various salary
levels, produced by the management consultants Hay-MSL.   It shows
that fringes expanded, relative to salary, from 1974 to 1978, particularly at very high salary levels.

While these figures confirm our general conclusion, they must be
treated with some care.   The valuation of major fringes like pensions and company cars requires assumptions which have not been
stated.   However, other figures in Table 2.24, produced by the
government's Top Salary Review Body with explicit assumptions,
suggest again that total fringes for the higher paid were increasing.
And these figures may even be underestimates, since they make conservative assumptions about the (growing) private use of company cars
and estimate pension values towards the lower end of the possible
range.

Table 2.23   Total Fringe Benefits, By Job Level

Job Level	Cost to employer of superannuation and fringe benefits as percentage of average salary plus bonus etc. before tax					Average pre tax salary plus bonus
	July 1974*	July 1975	July 1976	July 1977	July 1978	1978
Factory Superintendant	17	18	21	22	18	7,560
Works Manager	23	23	26	29	29	13,390
Manufacturing Manager	25	26	29	31	33	19,090
General Manager	16	26	29	31	37	23,510
Managing Director	12	29	33	35	36	30,240

Source: Royal Commission on the Distribution of Income and Wealth,
          Fourth Report, Cmnd. 7595.
*   1974 subject to error

Table 2.24   Total Fringe Benefits Ratio For Top
                         Managers

		Total fringe benefits as proportion of salary plus bonus (%)
1973	MBM	25
	SE	21
1977	MBM	28.4
	SE	24

Calculated from sources as for Table 2.20:   see Footnote 10.

It is difficult to say just how much the official income data is in-
complete at every level, and hence it is impossible to compute
exactly how much our inequality measures, would in practice be
raised by a proper evaluation.   Such an exercise awaits a decision
from the official statisticians to collect the appropriate data.
The evidence that is already available however, shows that existing
income inequality data are increasingly misleading.

Summary
We conclude this chapter by briefly summarising the main stylised
facts that have emerged from our detailed examination of diverse
sources of data.   These observations then form the empirical background for our attempt to explain the determinants of fringes which
begins in the next chapter.

I: Growth: All fringes have grown substantially over the last two
decades, and most have grown considerably faster than wages and
salaries.   The more valuable fringes, pension and paid holidays,
have risen steadily - in the former case because contributions and

expected benefits were raised, in the latter because almost every-
one has been getting longer holidays.   During the 1970s private use
of company cars grew especially fast and has now joined the ranks of
the major fringe benefits.   Subsidised services and other welfare
benefits are worth rather less.   They grew less fast on the whole,
except that private medical insurance took off rapidly in the late
1970s.   Benefits in kind are worth less still and have remained a
roughly constant proportion of wages.

II: Distribution: Most types of fringe benefit are much more unequally distributed than income.   Occupational pension schemes are
more widespread amongst the higher paid, and worth more to them.
At the extremes, for example the director of a large company, they
are worth at least 30% and possibly much more on top of salary.
Even more unequal is the private usage of company cars - worth up-
wards of 27% of salary for the average executive who gets one, while
hardly any of the lower paid receive this benefit.   Paid holidays,
however, are much more evenly distributed, though in 1981 there
remained some difference between non-manual and manual workers holiday lengths, and also lower paid workers typically receive a lower
proportion of normal pay while on holiday.

Many of the other benefits are also quite unequal, but these have
quantitatively less impact on the overall distribution of remuneration.   Company loans, payments of children's school fees, separate
life assurance and company share schemes may be quite valuable to an
employee who receives any such benefits (who tend to be highly paid),
but the numbers are relatively small compared even to the high paid
population.   Benefits in kind are quite widespread, and non-manual
workers do better, but they remain only of low value compared to
wages.   Finally private medical insurance is, not surprisingly,
most valuable and most widespread for high paid workers: but as yet
the cost of this to employers is not substantial in relation to
wages and salaries.

Footnotes

1. For detailed definitions, see Employment Gazette, May 1983.

2. Data from Green (1982), and Economic Trends, 1983.

3. Dunn and Hoffman (1983).

4. The Times, 28th September, 1983.

5. Potter (1983).

6. Potter and Cousins (1983).

7. Occupational and state pension rights have been integrated into wealth distribution data, showing a decrease in inequality (Dunn and Hoffmann, 1983). However, no one has yet tried to integrate the annual accrual of these rights into their measures of income inequality. It is interesting to note from their figures that between 1971 and 1980 the total wealth of private pensions grew by a factor of 5.5 compared to only 4.4 for the state sector. Taken all in all private and state pensions constitute an uneven distribution of rewards. A detailed analysis of related redistributional factors is given by Reddin.

8. Figures from Department of Health and Social Security (1977).

9. See Cunningham (1981) Ch. 3.

10. Appendix L of the REPORT, Cmnd 5846 and Appendix E of the SECOND REPORT, Cmnd 7253. The assumed split between business and private use was not stated in the case of the first report, but we suppose it is the same as the 50:50 split mentioned in the second.

11. These calculations are based on AA estimates of standing and running costs, assuming 8,000 miles per annum and under 18,000 business miles. The general manager is assumed to have a 2.5 litre car and the personnel executive a 1600 c.c. engine, and both on married man's allowance and receiving free petrol for private miles. Average salary estimates were taken from Inbucon (1982). Of course, not all managers receive free petrol or even free standing charges for private mileage and, in any case, company usage of a car will detract from both the real net value and the gross salary equivalent value of a car. Moreover, the tax liability of motoring on the company car has risen since 1982/83. However, even by 1984/85, with the arrival and consolidation of a 'free petrol' tax, the most a person could actually pay in tax is £1914 (corresponding to an added taxable income of £3190 at a marginal income tax rate of 60 per cent). For most company car users, the tax liability of

using a company car will be much less. The average general manager, in 1982 for example, would have paid about £270 in tax (for an item worth £4,000 in real net terms), that is, a tax rate of 6 per cent! Such figures were reinforced by Potter (1983) whose conservative estimates are that only 34% of the real benefit of large cars is assessable for tax, while for small cars it is a little higher at 43%.

12. Similar calculations have been made by the Institute of Directors (1983) who, in their survey of Directors' Rewards find that a director on a salary of around £25,000 per annum would require a further £11,000 in order to provide the net income which would cover the costs of a company car presently provided by the company.

13. Review Body on Top Salaries, Report No.16, Cmnd 8243. Since 1980 cost may well have increased.

14. Ibid.

15. Review Body on Top Salaries, Reports, Cmnd 7253 and Cmnd 8243.

16. See Atkinson (1983) for example.

17. Ibid., p.57. We assumed $\varepsilon = \frac{1}{2}$.

18. Economic Trends, May 1978 and February 1981.

APPENDIX: Further Data on Fringe Benefits

Table Al

MEAN HOLIDAY LENGTHS FOR MANUAL AND OFFICE WORKERS

	Manual Workers (Weeks)+	Office Workers, Basic entitlement (Weeks)++
1972	3.1	
1973	3.2	
1974	3.5	
1975	3.5	3.4
1976	3.6	3.6
1977	3.6	3.7
1978	3.6	3.7
1979	3.7	3.9
1980	4.1	4.1
1981	4.2	4.1
1982	4.4	4.3

+   D.E. Gazette

++   Alfred Marks Surveys, Actual holidays are longer due to service-related extra days.

Table A2

TRENDS IN PENSION BENEFITS AND CONTRIBUTIONS IN MANAGERIAL JOBS

| | Percentages | | | | | | | | |
	1970	1971	1972	1973	1974	1975	1976	1977	1978
Company Contributions range	3-25	3.5-25	3-25	3-25	3-25	3-31	4-31	0-38	3-42
average	7½	9	8	9	9	10	12	11	14
Employee Contribution range	2.5-7.5	2-8	2-8	2-9	2-9	1-8	1-9	2-9	2-9
average	n/a	4½	5	5	5	5	5	5	5
'Final Salary' as basis % of companies	84	87	90	90	91	94	96	99	98
% of companies on 1/60th benefit	70	73	77	83	84	90	91	85	91
Widow's Plan:									
Death in Service: % of companies	60	57	62	67	67	69	71	74	90

Source: Royal Commission on the Distribution of Income and Wealth:
Report No.3, Cmnd.6383 and Report No.7, Cmnd. 7595.

Table A3

HOLIDAYS IN DIFFERENT OCCUPATIONS, 1974 to 1981

| | Average Holidays Taken By Full-Time Workers | | | |
| | MALES | | FEMALES | |
OCCUPATIONS	1974	1981	1974	1981
MANUAL	3.40	4.37	3.25	4.17
NON-MANUAL	4.19	4.92	3.95	4.74
ALL	3.68	4.60	3.20	4.60
Some examples				
Professional and related supporting management and administration	4.17	4.77	3.92	4.55
Managerial (excluding general management)	4.32	5.06	3.64	4.74
Clerical and Related	3.83	4.55	3.43	4.28
Catering, cleaning, hairdressing and other personal service	3.24	4.34	3.27	n.a.
Farming, fishing and related	3.09	3.85	2.85	n.a.
Transport operating, materials, moving and storing and related	3.31	4.29	3.20	4.19

Source: Calculated from New Earnings Surveys, 1974 and 1981.

Table A4

VARIOUS FRINGES IN 1969

Quintiles of Household net disposable income	Mean Value of all Company Cars in Household as proportion of mean household income	Mean Value of meal vouchers and subsidised meals as proportion of mean household income	Proportion of employees provided with life assurance	Proportion of employees provided with free or subsidised goods and services
Top 20%	1.0	0.9	4.0	18.2
Second 20%	.5	1.1	2.8	19.3
Third 20%	.7	1.0	3.1	19.5
Fourth 20%	.5	1.2	0.8	16.3
Bottom 20%	.4	1.2	0	10.5

Source: Secondary analysis of Townsend's survey.

Table A5

AVERAGE PRICE OF CARS PROVIDED FOR MANAGERS, PRIVATE SECTOR (£)

| | 1973 | | 1980 | |
	Minimum	Maximum	Minimum	Maximum
Main Board Members	2,724	5,142	9,034	15,883
Senior Executives	1,930	2,611	6,580	10,037

Source: Review Body on Top Salaries, Report No.6, Cmnd. 5846,
Appendix E, and Report No.16, Cmnd. 8243.

Table A6

PRIVATE MEDICAL INSURANCE SCHEMES FOR CLERICAL WORKERS, % OF FIRMS

	Free	Discounted	None
1975			44
1976	10	45	45
1977	6	48	46
1978	7	43	50
1979	12	47	41
1980	19	38	43
1981	32	35	33
1982	34	35	31
1983	32	41	27

Source: Various Alfred Marks Surveys of Fringe Benefits for Office
Staff.

Table A7

LOANS AND FINANCIAL ASSISTANCE FOR HOUSE PURCHASE

| | 1973 | | 1977 | | 1980 | |
	Main Board Members	Senior Execu-tives	Main Board Members	Senior Execu-tives	Main Board Members	Senior Execu-tives
Annual Value of Loan, averaged over all re-spondents as proportion of remuneration (%)	0.2	1.0	0.4	0.7	n.a.	n.a.
Proportion of respondents in receipt of loan (%)	5.7	10.0	7.0	11.2	3.7	12.8
Average size of loan for those receiving one (£)	20,512	15,979	15,713	11,310	15,696	13,879
Average interest rate charged (%)	4.0	2.7	3.7	3.5	6.9	3.3

Source: Review Body on Top Salaries, Reports, Cmnd. 5846,
         Cmnd. 7253 and Cmnd. 8243.

Table A8

LOANS AND FINANCIAL ASSISTANCE FOR PURPOSES OTHER THAN HOUSE PURCHASE

	1973		1977		1980	
	Main Board Members	Senior Execu-tives	Main Board Members	Senior Execu-tives	Main Board Member	Senior Execu-tives
Annual Value of Loan, averaged over all re-spondents as pro-portion of re-muneration (%)	0.8	0.7	0.5	0.6	n.a.	n.a.
Proportion of respondents in receipt of loan (%)	7.8	11.6	6.7	9.5	5.0	7.5
Average size of loan for those receiving one (£)	28,096	9,233	13,276	7,415	5,029	4,372
Average interest rate charged (%)	1.4	1.3	6.7	9.5	3.1	4.3

Source: Review Body on Top Salaries, Reports, Cmnd.5846,
         Cmnd. 7253 and Cmnd. 8243.

Table A9

PROPORTIONS OF MANAGERS AND EXECUTIVES RECEIVING VARIOUS FRINGE
BENEFITS   (%)

Year	Full Use of Company Car	Subsidised Lunches	Life Assurance	Medical Insurance (Free)	Assistance With House Purchase	Low Interest Loans
1970	50.2	67.0	n.a	16.7	n.a.	n.a.
1971	54.6	66.1	n.a	17.5	n.a.	n.a.
1972	55.8	62.6	n.a.	17.3	n.a.	n.a.
1973	55.2	65.0	n.a.	26.4	6.3	n.a.
1974	62.0	64.2	75.3	30.1	4.7	n.a.
1975	60.6	63.6	83.4	37.9	6.4	n.a.
1976	62.3	67.3	81.3	37.3	5.9	7.2
1977	63.8	65.9	85.5	38.8	7.4	9.7
1978	67.4	68.6	89.1	44.1	8.0	9.6
1979	69.0	74.4	92.8	50.6	5.8	9.0
1980	72.4	71.3	90.9	57.9	6.3	7.0
1981	74.2	72.0	93.3	60.4	7.4	7.7
1982	77.7	71.0	92.4	63.0	6.7	6.5
1983	77.1	67.4	93.7	64.7	8.2	8.5

n.a.   not available

Source: Inbucon;   Management Surveys

Table A10

COMPANY SHARES

	1973		1977		1980	
	MBM	SE	MBM	SE	MBM	SE
Proportions receiving shares (%)	20.2	18.0	21.2	18.0	15.3[+]	9.9[+]
Average net benefit of shares acquired (£)	1,299	146	907	645	895	708
Net benefit averaged over all respondents as proportion of remuneration (%)	1.4	.3	.8	.8	n.a.	n.a.

+   These are maximum figures

Source: Review Body on Top Salaries, Reports, Cmnd. 5846,
          Cmnd. 7253 and Cmnd. 8243.

MBM: Main Board Members
SE: Senior Executives

CHAPTER 3

ECONOMIC THEORY

Introduction

A major theme which we pursue in this study is the unequal distribution of fringe benefits.   As we have shown in the last chapter, inequality in fringes is inevitably bound up with and tends to exceed
the inequality in wages.   The distribution of both types of remuneration can be understood in the context of the modern economic
thoery of labour markets.

To some extent wage differentials are explained by differences in the
individual skills acquired by workers.   Those workers who have been
able and chosen to undergo more training, whether general or job-
specific, can expect to receive more wages in a competitive world
where their extra skills can command a higher price in the market.
The same can be said of all aspects of jobs: higher quality workers
can demand better working conditions and higher fringe benefits.
But it is now widely recognised that the old neoclassical theory of
perfectly competitive labour markets with full information and
flexible labour prices and mobility across industries does not conform to reality.   A common theme of the marxist, institutionalist
and modern neoclassical approaches is that labour markets are, for
various reasons, substantially segmented with competition and movement across the various segments significantly restricted.   Thus
barriers to entry in labour markets contribute to the persistence of
income inequalities.   In the framework of segmented labour markets
(SLM) the basic distinction is between primary and secondary labour
markets.   Within the primary sector mobility is partially restricted by the setting up of internal labour markets.[1]

Our theory of fringe benefits derives partly as a by-product of SLM
theory, and partly from the cost advantages which some fringes enjoy
as a result of tax exemptions or economies of scale.   In brief, some
benefits (such as company cars) are simply explained by their enormous tax advantages, while with others there are additional or alternative factors to explain why they are paid.   Thus, given a favourable fiscal environment, and a system of work rewards with far from
perfect information, fringe benefits are an important means of setting
up and maintaining internal labour markets.   This approach enables
an understanding not only of why fringes are paid but also of why
they are unequally distributed and commonly share certain characteristics, such as being compulsory and associated with long job tenure.

As a matter of expositional convenience we have pigeon-holed the
various elements into supply-side and demand-side factors.   We
begin with the former, by examining fringes from the point of view
of management.   We then look at their value for workers especially
those who are employed in internal labour markets.   It should however be remembered that the two points of view are related.   If,
for example, a worker finds it advantageous for tax reasons to have
a certain amount of remuneration in the form of fringes it will also
be in managements interest to meet this demand, as it will reduce
unit labour costs.

The Supply of Fringes
If the managers of a firm decide to set up an internal labour market,
for whatever reason, they must attempt to deter workers from quitting.   A batch of devices exists for achieving this end.   Perhaps
the simplest is to pay more wages for workers with longer tenure.
Other strategies include agreeing to the 'Last-In-First-Out' principle in the case of lay-offs, thus rendering senior workers more
secure.   But the payment of fringes is a particularly useful device.

Certain types of fringes act as an especially effective economic
control mechanism: they inhibit turnover by imposing a relatively
large economic cost on quitters.   These are fringe benefits whose
payment increases with tenure more rapidly than wages do.   Such
'tenure-related' fringes include pension and sick pay rights as well
as paid holidays.   In extreme cases the costs are made so high that
workers have little choice other than to remain with the firm.
This is true of many Japanese workers, while older workers in Britain
with heavy pension rights to lose are often similarly entrapped
(Green, 1982b).   Even in less extreme cases, fringes are used as an
automatic mechanism to help set up internal labour markets.

Fringes can be used in this way because it is difficult, if not impossible, for workers - particularly job applicants - to acquire
information about them.   This is not surprising, given the number
and range of benefits that may or may not be on offer.   Cunningham
(1981) identifies 21 different possible kinds of fringe benefits, and
on top of this there are other varying aspects of conditions of work.
Workers would not expect to know all about what is on offer and
generally they will concentrate on the wage offered in deciding
whether to accept a job.   Since it is costly to find out about non-
wage aspects, and since fringes are not worth nearly as much as
wages, potential workers will not trouble to find out about them.
This result follows from a simple search model, which when formal-
ised (Green, 1982a), shows that, if the costs of searching for fringe
benefits are above a critical amount relative to the expected level
of fringes, it pays to follow a single acceptance wage rule.   This
result is consistent with evidence that fringes do not play a part
in attracting labour, at least for less-than-high-paid workers.

However fringes do play a role in maintaining labour supply by deter-
ring quitting.   Workers already with a company are more aware of the

value of fringes, and are more likely to take them into account when deciding whether or not to quit. Because of tax-relief and other factors (see below) management may find it advantageous to make fringes a substantial proportion of tenured workers remuneration, so that they become the particular vehicle through which seniority benefits are obtained. Tenure-related fringes impose heavy penalty costs on quitting, but fringes for novices are of comparatively little value for management in attracting new workers. Hence one would expect the ratio of fringes to wages to be greater for workers with greater tenure. A consequence of this is that workers may find themselves more locked in to their company than they imagined when joining it initially. This is consistent with the expressions of surprise and almost indignation that from time to time have come from workers who quit and lose substantial pension rights.

In stressing the effect of lack of perfect information in producing disproportionately tenure-related fringes for most workers, an interesting corollary emerges: that higher paid workers, for whom the value of fringe benefits is appreciable compared to the cost of finding out about them, are more likely to take them into account at all stages including initially. Thus there is no particular reason, with these workers, why any seniority premiums should be channelled disproportionately through fringes. We would expect that fringes as a proportion of wages do not increase with tenure - or, at least, that the rate of increase is lower than for low paid workers. (Moreover, at least in the private sector, high-paid workers are more likely to come under what the institutionalists call the 'independent' primary sector of the labour market, where mobility is quite high, and seniority premiums may be relatively less important).

In addition to these purely economic factors underlying management strategies, it is worth noting that fringe benefits also can have a special _ideological_ value to the firm. They can convey the spirit of the good employer who cares for the workers' needs. This generates loyalty to the company, and helps to lessen worker solidarity. Their value is very apparent to the Japanese manager who attempts to generate 'company workers' through the lifetime employment system. In Britain a whole range of fringes, from pensions and sick pay through to company sports and social facilities, can perform this ideological role.

This does not necessarily have to be part of a typical SLM strategy of the type we have described. It follows also from a paternalistic strategy which may be a declining form for the employer-worker relationship but which still exists. This is a mode of control in which deference to the paternalistic manager is combined with a high degree of worker attachment to and identification with the firm. Such deference is said to be 'traditional' and is characterised both by a recognition of class differences between worker and boss and by a perceived unity of interests; (Norris, 1978, Newby, 1977, Lawson, 1981). An essential aspect of this relationship is that the employer cares for the welfare of the worker, so that particular

42

fringe benefits will be important, and, given that paternalism typically goes also with low wages, fringes will be especially high in
proportion to wages.   Examples may be found in the histories of
Pilkingtons, Cadburys and Unilevers, which firms were typical early
providers of pension funds and other welfare schemes.   And at Pye of
Cambridge, Lawson (1981) notes that the largely female workforce
were provided with free or subsidised transport to and from work,
creche facilities at work and other welfare benefits not widely
found in modern post-war companies.   Part of the secret of this
mode of control lay in the ability to keep down the size of plant.

As 'traditional' authority has become gradually displaced, given the
pace of technology and changing markets, paternalism has declined
and is probably not a widespread form in Britain.   However, it is
not extinct, and may still be important in places with distinct
(isolated) local labour markets, where plant sizes are not too big,
and where the labour force is fairly easily subject to the ideology
of the company's paternalism.   It is possible also that paternalist
relations are more likely with a largely female labour force, as
prevailed at Pye.

Where it exists, paternalism may also break the SLM theory's usual
association of oligopolistic product markets with the primary sector
of the labour market.   Thus, a large company with a high market
share may still opt for secondary sector job characteristics: that
is, little skill and no job ladders or promotions.   So large firms
(even multi-nationals) or small ones might choose a paternalist
strategy if the conditions were right - implying no particular
relation between company size or degree of concentration with fringe
benefits.   In so far as paternalistic forms remain important these
comments qualify our main conclusions about the relationship between
internal labour market characteristics and fringes.

The Demand for Fringes
We now examine the advantages of fringe benefits from the point of
view of workers.   The most basic and obvious reason why they are
acceptable to some extent is that they are cheaper - that is, the
extra wages which employers could pay (for a given unit labour cost)
if they provided no fringes, would be insufficient to buy the same
amount of benefits on the open market.   Mainly, this is because
many fringes are favoured by the tax system.   Pension schemes,
luncheon vouchers, holidays, various physical benefits in kind
including company cars, and some subsidised services such as private
medical insurance, are all substitutes for higher wages which are
not subject to equivalent amounts of taxation.   Without any overall
consistent rationale successive British governments have supported
fringe benefits both by providing these tax concessions and by not
interfering with the tendencies towards segmentation in labour
markets (for example, nothing was done to limit the quit penalties
implicit in pension schemes; Green, 1982b).   We discuss these
government policies in some detail in Chapter 8, but for the present
we take the tax advantages as given.

The demand by workers for fringe benefits can be formally analysed
with the following simple model, depicted in Figure 1. Workers
choose between wage-goods, bought with wages, and fringe-benefit
goods which may either be supplied by the firm or bought with wages
on the open market. We assume for the purposes of this model that
workers have full information. The line LM represents the budget
constraint for a worker, given a certain level of remuneration and
no tax concessions.   The points A, B and C show three alternative
equilibria for workers with differing preferences (each buying
different quantities of fringes according to their preference
schedules).

Figure 1

Fringe
Benefit
Goods

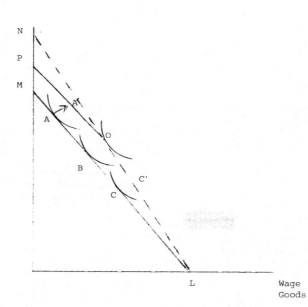

                                                            Wage
                                                            Goods

If the government subsidises fringe benefits by means of tax reliefs,
the new budget line would become LON assuming the firm's labour cost
is unchanged and it conferred with each worker over how much fringes
to supply.   Since, however, it is more likely that the firm will be
constrained to supply an equal amount of fringes to all workers on a
given level of remuneration (in the case of canteens, pensions and so
on) it must choose to match the preferences of as many workers as
possible.   If it matched the desires of worker B (the 'average'
worker), it would supply fringes at a point O - that point which max-
imises B's utility on LON.   Now, the overall workers' budget constraint is PO: extra fringes may be bought with wages, but the
fringes surplus to requirements of type C workers cannot normally be

44

resold on the open market.   The extent to which LO is steeper than
LM depends on the amount of the tax exemption and on the marginal
tax rate of the worker.

Within the new scenario, B is clearly better off and so prefers this
allocation of fringes.   A is also better off, but would decide to
supplement his fringe benefits from his wages and reach a point such
as A'.   C by contrast, is unable to move to a point such as C';
constrained to be at the point O, he or she may be better off but
could even be made worse off, depending on the shape of the indiff-
erence curve.

This standard analysis shows that the cost advantages of collective
provision have to be balanced against the advantages of giving each
the freedom to choose their preferred level.   It leads to the proposition that the demand for fringe benefit goods depends on the
level of cost advantage gained through government subsidy, the level
of the average worker's preferences for fringe benefits and, third,
the dispersion of these preferences.   The lower the dispersion
(that is, the more uniform their needs) the greater the likelihood
that firms supply them.

To this analysis, three points may be added.   First, the demand for
fringe benefits may or may not be income elastic.   Some fringes, for
example subsidised lunches, are more reasonably regarded as necess-
ities, while others, for example pension benefits, might come into
the category of luxuries.   Whichever effect turns out to be more
important is an empirical question.   But second, the higher the
level of wages and hence of income the higher is likely to be the
marginal tax rate.   The slopes of the relevant parts of the budget
lines are affected by the marginal tax rate.   Hence higher wages
lead to a greater proportion of fringe benefits to the extent that it
implies a greater cost advantage.

A third factor also influences the cost advantage.   It is sometimes
argued that firms can use economies of scale to provide fringe benefits cheaply.   This enables large firms to do better than small ones.
However, it is not obvious why large firms should necessarily perform
such functions more effectively than external competitive suppliers
of fringes direct to workers.   One possibility is that the marginal
cost of providing fringe benefits may be smaller for the firm that
employs the workers;   furthermore there is no uncertainty as far as
the scale of provision is concerned.   To the extent that the price
advantage is significant, this should also increase the proportion of
fringe benefits.

To complete the analysis of the demand for fringe benefits we must
however look beyond the level of the individual with full knowledge
in a single time period.

To begin with, many workers are in unions.   Apart from the general
expectation that unions represent workers preferences, we note that

unions are also an important institutional force in the setting up of internal labour markets. As Gordon, Reich and Edwards (1982) note, the segmentation of the US labour market was in response to growing union power in the 1930s. In so far as fringes are an aspect of internal labour markets, we would expect some positive relation between union power in the past and fringe benefits now. But this is a broad generalisation, and the precise effect on fringes would seem to depend on a complex and dynamic balance of forces.

A more specific argument has been developed by Mabry (1973). He maintains that unions have a disproportionate predilection to bargain for high fringe benefits since they are said to be more 'visible'. That is, unions gain the allegiance of workers by negotiating fringes more effectively than by negotiating an equivalent monetary gain in wages. Moreover, as Freeman (1981) observes, unions will be more efficient at negotiating complicated fringe benefit packages than non-union individuals. Additionally, unions are more likely to represent the interests of infra-marginal workers who are less mobile and who may have relatively greater preferences for fringes.

Whatever the validity of these arguments in the US context, the links in the UK between fringes and unions may be much less important. Here the unions have traditionally been stronger but they have often been distrustful of management-initiated fringe benefit schemes as being attempts to wean the allegiance of workers away from the union and towards the company. Moreover UK unions have been stronger than their US counterparts at the political level, partly through their connection with the Labour Party. Thus, they have generally pressed for the setting up and expansion of state welfare benefits, and, naturally, this tended to reduce any demands for private welfare schemes. As a result fringe schemes (such as pensions) were usually initiated by management rather than being granted in response to union demands. The one main exception to this may have been longer paid holidays, which have been pressed for by unions for many decades. It is only recently that UK unions have begun to take an interest in a wider variety of fringe benefits.

Footnotes

1. For a modern account, see Gordon, Edwards & Reich (1982), Wilkinson, (1982). For a classic statement of the institution-alists view, see Doeringer and Piore (1971), and of the radical view, Gordon, (1972). Rubery (1978) summarises the various theories and considers their applicability to the United King-dom. For a lucid account and an excellent survey of the modern neoclassical viewpoint see Okun (1981), Chapters 2 and 3.

CHAPTER 4

EMPIRICAL IMPLICATIONS
AND PREVIOUS STUDIES

Introduction

The theoretical argument of Chapter 3 suggested a number of factors which may be important determinants of fringe benefits. In this chapter we draw out some specific implications and examine how far they have been confirmed by previous studies in this area. This will pave the way for presenting our own results in the subsequent chapters. Most of the rather limited evidence to date has been based on United States labour markets and even there some questions are by no means adequately answered. We are primarily concerned here with the variation in the receipt of fringe benefits over and above the variation of wages, so that we take the level of fringes in relation to wages as the object to be explained. Normally this is measured as the simple ratio of the value of fringes to wages, or, where that is not available, by the probabilities of receiving each fringe benefit.[1]

Our principle aim is to find out which are the important factors, rather than to test any particular theory of labour markets. In so far as the implications of the last chapter are broadly confirmed, this will at least be consistent with the segmented labour market/fiscal environment approach. But beyond this we do not attempt to discriminate empirically between the neoclassical and the radical explanations of that framework.

The Main Factors
(i) Wages

We expect that higher wages will be associated with a higher fringe benefits share. For one thing, relatively high wages are thought to be a feature of the primary labour market, as also is a high share of fringes. Hence we expect the two to be correlated, even though this is not to argue that high wages 'cause' a high fringe share. In this sense relatively high wages are just another indicator of the likely importance of internal markets. However, independently of any segmentation in the labour market, wages may cause a higher fringe share either because worker's demands for fringe benefits are income elastic, or because higher wages imply a higher marginal tax rate and hence a lower relative cost of (untaxed) fringes.

There is quite a lot of direct or indirect evidence on the effect of wages or of total compensation on the level of fringe benefits. But while it is widely agreed that higher wages leads to higher absolute fringes, there is no clear conclusion as to whether the income elasticity of fringes is less or greater than 1. In the US, Rice (1966) quotes evidence from cross-sectional surveys that the elasticity is greater than 1 and this is confirmed by Solnick (1978) and Woodbury (1983 and 1981). The latter attempted to distinguish between the income elasticity of demand for fringes and the wage effect that goes through the tax saving, finding that in addition to the tax effect the income elasticity is more than 1. Viscusi (1979) found that the probability of fringe benefit coverage increases significantly with earnings and that this was so for overall fringes, medical insurance, life insurance and pensions. Freeman (1981), however, found an income elasticity of 0.96. As for UK evidence, Reid and Robertson (1965) found that the ratio of fringe costs to payroll was, if anything, slightly negatively correlated with wages. However, Hawkesworth (1978) found an elasticity above 1, and this is consistent with the findings of Townsend (1979) and others, as collected together in the various tables of chapter 2 above, that the distribution of income including fringe benefits is more unequal than the distribution of wages and salaries on their own.

(ii) Tenure

Our theory suggested that long job tenure is associated with a high relative share of certain types of fringes. Some schemes are specifically designed to be tenure-related in order to induce employees to stay longer in the job. Thus the causation may run in both directions. Whether or not this incentive makes any difference to tenure, the long-serving worker will thereby have relatively high fringes given that such schemes exist. However, our consideration of the role of information led us to the expectation that the correlation of fringes with tenure would not necessarily apply to the minority of highly remunerated workers.

Many previous researchers have not addressed themselves to this issue, but there is immediately the casual and familiar evidence in the UK that many workers have elements of their holiday and sick pay entitlements related to service, while pension schemes are well known to impose penalties on early leavers.

There is some indirect evidence on the relevance of the 'search' approach in that, as expected, fringe benefits do not seem to have an effect on labour supply decisions of most new workers (though they may affect quitting, see below). For a start, it has not been found helpful to include them as an argument in labour supply functions, though this could be because no one has yet seriously tried to estimate their effect. As for the effect of fringes on the labour supply of high paid workers, which our hypothesis suggests should be more important, there is no previous systematic evidence. However it may be observed that they do figure heavily in advertisements for high paid jobs.

For the majority of workers whenever they have been examined in a more systematic way it has emerged that fringe benefits play less of a role in attracting labour than they do in retaining it later. Such was the conclusion of Reid and Robertson (1965) for Britain, and this was echoed by Lester (1967) for the US. More recent evidence for manual workers in Britain (Blackburn and Mann, 1979) confirmed that fringe benefits only rarely influenced a decision whether to accept or refuse a job. However there is some convincing evidence from abroad (mainly US) that some fringe benefits do have a significant impact on labour mobility. Using 1960s data on individuals, Schiller and Weiss (1979) and Lurie (1965), found that non-vested pensions had a significant negative effect on quitting, and this is strongly confirmed by Bartel (1982). Merrilees (1981) used job tenure as the dependent variable and found that fringes - especially pensions - had a significant positive effect, greater in his 1973 data set than in the 1968 set, and he suggests that increasing awareness of the costs of job changing contributed to the enhanced effect in the 1970's. Mitchell (1981) confirms that pensions and medical insurance significantly decreased quitting in the 1970's, though other fringes had no significant impact. In fact, she computes that on average medical insurance increases job changing costs roughly 3½ times while pensions increase them by as much as a factor of 7. Viscusi (1979) using data from the University of Michigan Survey of Working Conditions, 1969-70, finds that fringe benefit coverage reduces substantially the quit intention probability. Finally, Matsukawa (1977) has found evidence of a similar deterrent effect on quitting in Japan.

In Britain, studies of labour mobility are limited, and only Curran (1981) to our knowledge attempts to measure the impact of fringes. We think this is invalid. Her study, based on MLH industry as the observation unit, investigates the impact of industry variables on turnover and quit rates. She found a significant negative coefficient of fringe benefit costs on turnover, but this evidence must be heavily qualified for at least two reasons. First, she did not have separate fringe benefit cost data for each MLH unit and used instead the average level for the Industry Order as published in the labour cost surveys in the Employment Gazette. Second, since some fringes are tenure-related, it is clear that, whether or not they have a deterrent effect on quitting, fringe benefit costs will be high in those industries where tenure is relatively high (and presumably turnover on the low side). Hence the observed negative coefficient on fringe costs is not evidence of a deterrent effect.

(iii) Size

Greater size of establishment or firm is likely to increase the proportion of fringes, including that of tenure-related fringes. This is so for two reasons: first, small firms are relatively less likely to adopt an internal labour market strategy and hence to attempt to induce long-term worker-employer relationships; second, there may be economies of scale in the provision of fringes.

Paternalistic firms provide a possible qualification to this argument, since paternalism tends to thrive better in smaller establishments, yet it involves a heavy element of fringe benefits. However, such strategies are relatively uncommon, and we do not expect this to cancel the expected positive association of size with fringes. A negative association would only show up in a few individual case studies where paternalism is important.

Previous studies provide some support for our expectation, but no adequate evidence for the UK economy. Reid and Robertson's (1965) study in Glasgow of fringe benefits in 1960, found no evidence of any correlation with size, but this excluded companies with less than 50 workers. However, for the US, Rice (1966) reports a significant positive effect of size, and this is confirmed more recently by Solnick (1978), Woodbury (1981), Freeman (1981) and Woodbury (1983).

(iv) Type of Worker
Different types of workers are to be found in different types of labour markets and hence we expect them to vary in the fringe shares they receive. For example, it is possible that management would be more likely to set up internal labour markets for certain non-manual groups than for manual groups. If manual workers require little or no skills for their work as is now often the case (Blackburn and Mann, 1979), secondary labour market conditions may be more likely. Moreover, there remain ideological differences in attitudes towards manual and non-manual work despite the obvious changes in many non-manual occupations (eg. clerical work) which have rendered them increasingly like factory jobs; (Braverman, 1974). These can mean different expectations about the nature of work and the sorts of conditions that surround them - hence also of fringes.

Townsend (1979) offers an additional hypothesis as to why manual workers fringes may be less than those of non-manuals. His view of the labour market puts the emphasis on pre-market segmentation, in particular on the influence on income of occupational class structure. He argues that empirically the clearest segmentation in the UK lies between manual and non-manual workers, and observes that this is particularly true of fringes. His thesis is that fringes play a role in maintaining and reinforcing inequality. Management's strategy is to avoid too great a perception of inequality by low paid workers, and he suggests that fringes are not so open because they do not (usually) enter into a collective bargain. Hence, fringes are relatively high for non-manual workers as a way of concealing from manual workers the true extent of the differential. This thesis is somewhat implausible in the case of some fringes - for example, company cars, separate management canteens and so on - which are consumed partly at work: they are if anything more visible than the wage differences, not less. But it may be more sound in the case of pensions and some other fringes where the details of the benefit schemes on offer are complex, partly concealed and difficult to follow without great effort even by long-serving workers.

51

Other divisions between workers may also affect fringes. For example, we would expect that the full-time worker is more likely to be attached long term to a firm than a part-timer; moreover the costs of administration of fringes might be relatively high for those who only work a few hours. For these reasons we expect part-timers to do worse than full-timers in terms of fringes.

Finally, firms may sometimes adopt different strategies depending on the sex composition of their labour force. It is usually suggested that female workers tend to be concentrated in secondary labour markets. That is, 'being female' is in this context an indicator of likely labour market status, and for this reason we would expect that, ceteris paribus, male workers' fringe benefits are greater on average than those of females. This effect also is qualified by the possible role of paternalism which may be more prevalent with female labour forces.

The existing evidence on these hypotheses is however very sparse. Although it is clear from a number of sources (eg. Townsend, 1979; Murlis, 1974; Diamond Commission, Report No. 7, Cmnd. 7595) that on average men fare better than women, non-manuals than manuals and full-time than part-time employees, this evidence is unsatisfactory as it does not take into account the independent effect on other variables, especially wages. Thus non-manuals fringes could be better than those of manuals simply because their incomes are higher. Hawkesworth (1978) accounts for this in a limited way, but his regression evidence was based on only 19 aggregated observations: he found that in Britain being non-manual and/or female significantly increased the share of fringes.

(v) Union Membership
We ended the last chapter with the arguments that unions tended to influence positively the fringe share in the US but that in the UK their direct influence may be less strong. Not surprisingly, all the evidence on this matter so far has come from the US - no one has yet looked for any influence in Britain.

In the US Rice (1966) found no significant effect of unionisation, and a recent study, Feldman and Scheffler (1982), of the effect of unions on wages and fringe benefits for hospital workers is inconclusive. However, Lester (1967), Lawler and Levin (1968), Leigh (1981), Mabry (1972), Freeman (1981), Woodbury (1981, 1983) and Solnick (1978) all confirm that unions increase the proportion of remuneration paid for in fringes. Also Kalamotousakis (1972) finds that unionisation increases the level of pension expenditure while a significant effect of unionisation on the probability of fringe coverage was found by Viscusi (1979). Gustman and Segal (1972) argued that the effect of unions worked through imitation, i.e. fringe benefits in one contract were influenced by the level negotiated in similar contracts in the locality. However, it is not clear that their evidence supports their proposition. A curious exception to this near unanimity is the evidence of Feuille et al

(1981), which suggests that unions tilt compensation packages towards wages and so away from the non-wage aspects of contracts.
In their case, non-wage conditions include non-pecuniary characteristics of jobs as well as fringes, which taken together with the
other evidence suggests, rather surprisingly, that unions on
balance are relatively less concerned about job conditions.

(vi) Other Factors

The theory also suggests a number of factors which could be
important, for which there is no previous evidence. For example,
according to the SLM approach, where there are high job-specific
skills there are likely to be internal labour markets and hence high
fringes. For lack of appropriate data on skills we see no immediate prospect of testing such a hypothesis. However, there are
certain characteristics of an industry which <u>are</u> measurable and
which may be a clue to the likelihood of high or low fringes. For
example, it is sometimes argued that industries with highly concentrated and reasonably stable product markets are more likely to go
for a primary labour market strategy (though Lawson, 1981, correctly
points to the possibility of exceptions to this rule, particularly
for paternalistic firms). These, and other factors such as the
level of unemployment, will be considered below in Chapter 6 where
we make use of industry-level data.

Methodology

Our own empirical investigations, the results of which are reported
in the following chapters, aim to clarify the importance in the UK
labour market of many of the factors listed above.

There is no single adequate data set on fringe benefits in Britain,
but there is a variety of sources of information. There are the
Department of Employment's Labour Cost Surveys of businesses,
various management surveys mainly on higher paid employees, Alfred
Marks Surveys for the fringes of office staff, some surveys by the
British Institute of Management, and a number of other official
surveys with relevant data, (including the General Household Survey
and the New Earnings Survey) and the Poverty Survey carried out by
Townsend in 1969.

All these data sources have their limitations. It is regrettable
that despite their growing importance an adequate single source of
fringe benefit data has not yet been financed by successive governments. Nonetheless, it is an advantage that there are several
quite distinct data sources, for this allows some results to be
cross-checked and hopefully confirmed. Our procedure in this book
is to use the different sources to obtain what systematic evidence
can be had from each. We then build up a consistent picture as far
as is possible. As we shall show below, this approach turns out to
be fruitful and we are able to shed light in the UK context on many
though not all of the specific hypotheses developed in this chapter.

Footnotes

1. All the hypotheses listed in this chapter would apply equally
    to the ratio of fringes to total labour costs, which is argu-
    ably the more appropriate variable from the employer's point of
    view.

2. A 'vested' pension right is one where the benefit is guaranteed
    after a person quits a job.

CHAPTER 5

THE DISTRIBUTION OF FRINGES: I

It is usually more satisfactory, where possible, to work with information about individuals or households rather than with industry-level
data (however disaggregated), and in this chapter we begin our report
by presenting results based on cross-section data from the General
Household Survey (GHS) of 1976 and Townsend's Poverty Survey conducted in 1969.   In Chapter 6 we analyse the distribution of fringes
across industries, and summarise our overall conclusions regarding
distribution before proceeding to consider the question of growth in
Chapter 7.

Results from the General Household Survey, 1976
The GHS collected information regarding sick pay and pension scheme
membership until 1976.   The only other fringe benefit it covered
was accommodation which was much less widespread.   In all three
cases our dependent variable was a univariate dichotomous variable
taking values of one or zero corresponding to answers of yes or no
to the questions: "do you get sick pay from your employer?";   "do
you belong to an employers' private pension scheme?";   and finally,
"do you live in accommodation linked to your job?".   Our aim was to
explain the replies to these questions as far as possible in terms
of a subset of independent variables from the GHS.

Table 5.1 gives a list of variables used in our multiple regression
analysis, based on the Linear Probability Model (LPM).   Thus we
estimated the probability of receiving each of the three fringes.
To cover all cases, up to 72 dummy variables were specified.   Since
we were concerned with fringe benefits provided by definition with
employment, the full sample was reduced to one that excluded house-
wives, children, the retired, self-employed persons and the unemployed.   This resulted eventually in a sub-sample of 7317 observations -
a number which varied marginally depending on the variables included
at any one time.

The Linear Probability Model suffers from a number of shortcomings,
in terms of the properties of the estimators employed.   But its use
may be rationalised (Pindyck and Rubinfeld, 1981) by pointing out,
first, its low computational cost and, second, the observation from a
number of studies and Monte Carlo exercises that "... the estimated
parameters obtained from the linear probability models and the maximum likelihood logit estimators are usually the same" (p.294).
These considerations are particularly relevant in our case given the

Table 5.1   GHS Independent Variables

	Label	Category
(a) Sex	DS	Male
	RC*	Female
(b) Age	DA1	25-35 yrs
	DA2	35-45 yrs
	DA3	45-55 yrs
	DA4	55-65 yrs
	DA5	65-75 yrs
	DA6	Aged 75 and over
	RC*	Under 25 years
(c) Social Class	DC1	Employers and Managers
	DC2	Intermdte and Jun. Non-Man.
	DC3	Skilled Manual
	DC4	Semi-skilled Manual etc.
	DC5	Unskilled Manual
	DC6	Armed Forces
	RC*	Professional
(d) Standard Indust-rial Classi-fication (1968)	D 1	Mining & Quarrying
	D 2	Food, Drink & Tobacco
	D 3	Coal & Petroleum Products
	D 4	Chemical & Allied Industries
	D 5	Metal Manufacture
	D 6	Mechanical & Electrical Engineering
	D 7	Instrument Engineering
	D 8	Shipbuilding and Marine Engineering
	D 9	Textiles
	D10	Leather goods, fur, etc.
	D11	Clothing and Footwear
	D12	Bricks, Cement, Pottery, etc.
	D13	Timber and Furniture, etc.
	D14	Paper, Printing and Publishing
	D15	Other Manufacturing
	D16	Construction
	D17	Gas, Electricity and Water
	D18	Transport and Communication
	D19	Wholesale and Retail
	D20	Insurance, Banking, etc.
	D21	Professional and Scientific Services
	D22	Miscellaneous Services
	D23	Public Admin. and Defence
	RC*	Agriculture, Forestry and Fishing
(e) Tenure	DTEN1	3 to 12 months in job
	DTEN2	1 to 5 years in job
	DTEN3	Over 5 years in job
	RC*	Under 3 months in job

	Label	Category
(f) Earnings	DI 1	£500-£1000 per annum
	DI 2	£1000-£1500 per annum
	DI 3	£1500-£2000 per annum
	DI 4	£2000-£2500 per annum
	DI 5	£2500-£3000 per annum
	DI 6	£3000-£3500 per annum
	DI 7	£3500-£4000 per annum
	DI 8	£4000-£5000 per annum
	DI 9	£5000-£6000 per annum
	DI10	£6000-£7000 per annum
	DI11	Over £7000 per annum
	RC*	Under £500 per annum
(g) Highest	DE 1	Higher Degrees
Educational	DE 2	1st Degree or Univ. Dip.
Qualifications	DE 3	Non grad. Teaching Qual.
	DE 4	HNC/HND/Technical Cert.
	DE 5	Nursing Qualification
	DE 6	GCE 'A' levels, OND, etc.
	DE 7	GCE 'O' levels, (5 and over)
	DE 8	GCE 'O' levels (1-4) and CCQ
	DE 9	GCE 'O' levels (1-4) no CCQ
	DE10	Clerical and Commercial Qual.
	DE11	CSE, Other
	DE12	Apprenticeship
	DE13	Any Foreign Qual.
	DE14	Other Qual.
	DE15	Don't know/no answer
	DE16	'O' levels, but don't know number
	DE17	Still in full-time education
	RC*	No Qualifications
(h) Hours	DH1	Under 11 hours per week
Worked	DH2	11 to 21 hours per week
	DH3	31 to 41 hours per week
	DH4	41 to 51 hours per week
	DH5	Over 51 hours per week
	RC*	21 to 31 hours per week

*RC = Reference Category

dimensions of our observations matrix both in terms of the number of
the variables used and the number of observations on each variable.

The likelihood of a 'yes' answer to the above questions is expected
to depend on a number of considerations, most of which follow directly from the discussion of the last chapter.   Thus the inclusion of
earnings, length of job tenure, social class (as measured by occupation), hours worked and sex variables require no further comment.
An industry dummy was used as this was the only way of capturing
particular unspecified conditions and traditions.   Our other variables are by no means perfect indices of labour market characteristics in each industry.   In addition, we wanted to examine whether
workers in industries dominated by the public sector were more
likely to be treated well in terms of 'welfare' fringes: this was a
possibility if for historical reasons the state enterprises felt the
need to appear as model employers.   An 'Age' variable was used
because older workers might have different preferences from younger
ones, and hence value more highly certain fringes which are somehow
associated with age, such as pensions, medical insurance, and sick
pay;   finally, they are on the whole less mobile than younger workers.
The inclusion of educational attainment is more speculative: it is
an attempt to find out whether employees with a higher level of formal education are more likely to participate in a pension or a sick
pay scheme or to have an accommodation linked with their job because
they may be more aware of their existence and importance;   or
because they expect to have a job that provides these benefits.

(i)   Entitlement to Sick Pay:
Our first regression seeks to explain the workers probability of en-
titlement to sick pay.   The full set of results are reported in
Table 5.2.

While sex is not at all significant, the estimated probability of
entitlement to sick pay rises with age until a peak for the age group
45 to 55.   However, over the age of 65 (as one might expect) there
is much less chance of receiving sick pay.   Although the only coefficient to be significant at the 95% confidence level is on the
dummy for the 45-55 age group, most of the remaining coefficients
have individual t-statistics of 1.35 and over and so they cannot be
dismissed.

The coefficients on the social class dummies are mostly negative.
This conforms to our expectations, given that the reference category
is 'professional'.   The results suggest clearly that manual workers
were less likely to belong to a sick pay scheme than 'professional'
workers.   In contrast, the incidence of this type of benefit seemed
to be higher among employers and managers.   The only unexpected
feature here is that unskilled manual workers seem to have a better
chance of benefitting from this form of remuneration than skilled
manual workers.

58

Table 5.2   Sickpay Entitlement

Summary Statistics: $\overline{R}^2$ = 0.283, n = 7317, F(70,7246) = 42.3

Standard Error = 0.396, Pr = 0.678
                        (Mean Value of Dependent Variable)

Independent Variables:

Label	Coefficient	Standard Error	Label	Coefficient	Standard Error
DS	-0.0066	0.0140	DTEN1	0.124**	0.0241
DA 1	0.022	0.0162	DTEN2	0.264**	0.0220
DA 2	0.032	0.0173	DTEN3	0.327**	0.0226
DA 3	0.036*	0.0178	DI 1	-0.021	0.0201
DA 4	0.029	0.0194	DI 2	0.072**	0.0199
DA 5	-0.025	0.0347	DI 3	0.118**	0.0202
DA 6	-0.154	0.0959	DI 4	0.115**	0.0197
DC 1	0.041	0.0304	DI 5	0.118**	0.0203
DC 2	-0.0095	0.0288	DI 6	0.128**	0.0217
DC 3	-0.234**	0.0295	DI 7	0.148**	0.0218
DC 4	-0.109**	0.0300	DI 8	0.116**	0.0348
DC 5	-0.132**	0.0339	DI 9	0.116**	0.0338
DC 6	-0.105	0.0672	DI10	0.094*	0.0469
D 1	0.064	0.0479	DI11	0.095	0.0490
D 2	0.045	0.0408	DE 1	0.056	0.0742
D 3	0.138	0.1019	DE 2	0.054	0.0322
D 4	0.109*	0.0469	DE 3	0.0051	0.0408
D 5	-0.132**	0.0462	DE 4	0.089**	0.0322
D 6	-0.105**	0.0352	DE 5	-0.0048	0.0474
D 7	0.093	0.0681	DE 6	0.102**	0.0220
D 8	-0.217**	0.0562	DE 7	0.037*	0.0182
D 9	-0.251**	0.0460	DE 8	0.138**	0.0450
D10	-0.277**	0.1019	DE 9	0.067**	0.0228
D11	-0.316**	0.0478	DE10	0.064*	0.0267
D12	-0.1822**	0.0548	DE11	0.045	0.0385
D13	-0.109	0.0634	DE12	0.065**	0.0220
D14	0.0033	0.0432	DE13	0.024	0.0509
D15	-0.106*	0.0484	DE14	0.041	0.0262
D16	-0.060	0.0372	DE15	-	-
D17	0.169**	0.0484	DE16	-0.136	0.1258
D18	0.101**	0.0372	DE17	-	-
D19	-0.054	0.0356	DH 1	-0.280**	0.0279
D20	0.043	0.0396	DH 2	-0.052*	0.0228
D21	0.132**	0.0357	DH 3	0.107**	0.0193
D22	0.015	0.0360	DH 4	0.073**	0.0251
D23	0.127**	0.0382	DH 5	0.045	0.0356

Constant   0.334

** significant at 99%
* significant at 95%

The incidence of this benefit is significantly influenced by the length of tenure. It would appear that, ceteris paribus, the probability of a worker with at least five years service being entitled to sick pay is 0.33 higher than the corresponding probability for a new worker (less than three months service). The importance of this factor in our analysis is fully reflected by the size and significance of all dummy coefficients on tenure.

Another unequivocal result is the significance of the length of the working week. The probability of entitlement rises with the number of hours worked peaking for those working the widespread 31-41 hours per week. Part-time workers are, therefore, worse off in this respect.

The regression suggests that income is an important factor in explaining the incidence of this benefit. The probability is highest for those in the income group £3500-£4000 and considerably lower for the low income-earners.

Although there is, on the whole, a greater likelihood of sick pay if one holds certain educational qualifications, the coefficients are significantly positive (at the 95 per cent probability level) on only seven out of fifteen educational dummies. Having, for example a higher educational qualification (eg. a university degree) does not seem to convey an advantage in this respect, relative to those with only GCE 'O' level results. But it is an advantage to have GCE passes rather than no qualifications at all. However the interpretation of this result is open to question.[1]

The coefficients on industry dummies conform broadly to our expectations. For example, working in Gas, Electricity and Water or Public Administration and Defence (ie. being employed by the state) considerably improves a worker's chance of receiving sick pay (vis-a-vis Agriculture, Forestry and Fishing) whereas working in Textiles, Leather Goods, Clothing and Footwear or Brick-making etc. reduces the corresponding probability.

The following - based on our regression results - illustrates the difference in the chances of employees with substantially different characteristics of belonging to a private sick pay scheme. The figures against the various characteristics of a worker are dummy regression coefficients as reported in Table 5.2. They indicate the estimated probability associated with each category of worker, as indicated below, in comparison with the reference or base categories which carry a zero coefficient (see Table 5.1). The overall estimated probability shows clearly that worker B is much more likely to belong to a private sick pay scheme than worker A.

Characteristic	Worker A		Worker B	
Sex	Male	-0.0066	Male	-0.0066
Age	Under 25	0.0000	35-45	0.0320
Social Class	Unskilled Manual	-0.1320	Professional	0.0000
Industry	Clothing & Footwear	-0.3160	Insurance	0.0430
Tenure	3-12 months	0.1240	1-5 years	0.2640
Income	£1000-£1500	0.0720	£3500-£4000	0.1480
Education	No qualifications	0.0000	1st Degree	0.0540
Hours per week	11-21 hours	-0.0520	31-41	0.1070
Constant of regression		0.3340		0.3340
Estimated Probability		0.0234		0.9754

In an effort to find out whether these factors retain their significance in explaining the incidence of this benefit among high income
earners, we ran the same regression only for those earning over
£4,500 p.a.   The relevant sample consists of 551 observations with
92% of the corresponding employees having a sick pay provision (the
equivalent figure for the full sample is only 67%).   The results
suggest that of the high income earners the few employees not
receiving sick pay are likely to be female, manual, part-time and
older (65+) employees.   Notably, tenure does not seem to be a relevant consideration, which conforms to our expectations (see Chapter
4).

(ii)   Private Pension Entitlement:
The main results of this type of benefit are reported in Table 5.3.
Only 47% of the individuals in our sample were receiving this benefit in contrast to 67% for sick pay.   In common with the findings
for sick pay these results suggest that income, tenure, social class,
the number of hours worked per week, industrial classification and
age are significant arguments in explaining the incidence of this
benefit.   In addition sex and high educational attainment also seem
to be significant here.[2]

The industry dummies indicate that the remuneration package of workers in Agriculture, Forestry and Fishing is less likely to include
this benefit than the package of nearly all other workers.   As with
sick pay, the public sector dominated industries are especially
important - Gas, Electricity and Water, Mining and Quarrying and
Public Administration and Defence have the highest coefficients.
Apart from this, the pattern of significant coefficients tends to
differ from those relevant for sick pay.

The following provides an illustration of the significance of the
various worker characteristics in explaining the presence or absence
of this benefit from a remuneration package.

Table 5.3   Private Pension Entitlement

Summary Statistics: $\overline{R}^2$ = 0.405, n = 7317, F(70,7246) = 72.1

Standard Error = 0.385,   Pr = 0.470
                           (Mean Value of Dependent Variable)

Independent Variables:

Label	Coefficient	Standard Error	Label	Coefficient	Standard Error
DS	0.082**	0.0136	DTEN1	0.035	0.0235
DA 1	0.099**	0.0158	DTEN2	0.146**	0.0214
DA 2	0.102**	0.0168	DTEN3	0.272**	0.0220
DA 3	0.145**	0.0174	DI 1	-0.104**	0.0196
DA 4	0.121**	0.0189	DI 2	-0.109**	0.0194
DA 5	-0.045	0.0338	DI 3	-0.012	0.0196
DA 6	0.010	0.0933	DI 4	0.096**	0.0192
DC 1	-0.021	0.0296	DI 5	0.128**	0.0197
DC 2	0.026	0.0280	DI 6	0.187**	0.0211
DC 3	-0.105**	0.0287	DI 7	0.204**	0.0212
DC 4	-0.055	0.0292	DI 8	0.249**	0.0339
DC 5	-0.969*	0.0329	DI 9	0.192**	0.0328
DC 6	-0.048	0.0654	DI10	0.195**	0.0456
D 1	0.358**	0.0466	DI11	0.212**	0.0477
D 2	0.187**	0.0397	DE 1	0.234**	0.0722
D 3	0.189	0.0991	DE 2	0.072*	0.0313
D 4	0.285**	0.0456	DE 3	0.319**	0.0397
D 5	0.185**	0.0450	DE 4	0.128**	0.0314
D 6	0.145**	0.0343	DE 5	0.142**	0.0462
D 7	0.112	0.0663	DE 6	0.102**	0.0214
D 8	0.180**	0.0547	DE 7	0.066**	0.0177
D 9	0.034	0.0448	DE 8	-0.015	0.0438
D10	0.090	0.0992	DE 9	0.048*	0.0222
D11	-0.0023	0.0466	DE10	-0.014	0.0259
D12	0.090	0.0533	DE11	-0.031	0.0375
D13	-0.132*	0.0617	DE12	0.016	0.0214
D14	0.190**	0.0421	DE13	0.066	0.0495
D15	0.150**	0.0471	DE14	0.071**	0.0255
D16	-0.042	0.0362	DE15	–	–
D17	0.290**	0.0471	DE16	-0.043	0.1224
D18	0.275**	0.0362	DE17	–	–
D19	0.045	0.0346	DH 1	-0.191**	0.0272
D20	0.197**	0.0386	DH 2	-0.117**	0.0226
D21	0.209**	0.0347	DH 3	0.142**	0.0188
D22	0.099**	0.0350	DH 4	0.089**	0.0244
D23	0.313**	0.0372	DH 5	0.023	0.0347

Constant   -0.139

**   significant at 99%
*   significant at 95%

Characteristic	Worker A		Worker B	
Sex	Female	0.0000	Male	0.0820
Age	25-35	0.0990	45-55	0.1450
Social Class	Unskilled Manual	-0.0690	Professional	0.0000
Industry	Clothing & Footwear	-0.0023	Insurance	0.1970
Tenure	1-5 years	0.1460	Over 5 years	0.2720
Income	£1000-£1500	-0.1090	£3500-£4000	0.2040
Education	Apprenticeship	0.0160	1st Degree	0.0720
Hours per week	31-41 hours	0.1420	31-41 hours	0.1420
Constant of regression		-0.1390		-0.1390
Estimated Probability		0.0837		0.9750

When only high income earners are used for the estimation of the regression for pension entitlement the results confirm our previous
findings. The incidence of this benefit for this group is very high
(86 per cent). The coefficients suggest that, even in this group,
young, part-time, skilled manual workers with low educational level
are less likely to receive this benefit, though the explanatory
power of the regression is very low (R^2 = 0.152). Tenure, however,
as expected is not significant.

(iii) Accommodation Linked with Job:
In terms of frequency of occurrence, this is a much less important
benefit than either sick pay or pension - only 4.3 per cent of the
sample of employees were receiving this benefit. The results are
reported in Table 5.4.

Despite the low explanatory power of the regression ($\overline{R}^2$ = 0.115) the
set of regressors taken together contributes signficantly in explaining the incidence of this benefit. However, the estimated coefficients suggest that fewer of the explanatory variable are relevant in
this case than before.

The results suggest, first, that younger workers, (those below 25),
those in the armed forces and those in the Agriculture, Forestry and
Fishing industry are relatively more likely to receive this benefit.
It is less likely to occur in higher income groups - this may reflect
a higher incidence for those providing domestic help of various
types, nannies, etc. Also it is a common benefit for farm workers
and nurses and those working very long hours (over 41, and especially
over 51 hours per week).

Although the coefficients on sex and tenure are not significant at
the 95 per cent level, they do suggest, at a lower confidence level,
that female and long-tenure workers are more likely to receive this
benefit.

Table 5.4   Accommodation Linked to Job

Summary Statistics: $\overline{R}^2$ = 0.115, n = 7317, $F(70,7246)$ = 14.5

Standard Error = 0.191, Pr = 0.043
                    (Mean Value of Dependent Variable)

Independent Variables:

Label	Coefficient	Standard Error	Label	Coefficient	Standard Error
DS	0.0090	0.0067	DTEN1	0.0093	0.0117
DA 1	-0.00080	0.0078	DTEN2	0.011	0.0106
DA 2	-0.016	0.0083	DTEN3	0.021	0.0110
DA 3	-0.019*	0.0086	DI 1	0.013	0.0097
DA 4	-0.028**	0.0094	DI 2	0.0035	0.0096
DA 5	-0.036*	0.0168	DI 3	-0.0062	0.0098
DA 6	-0.068	0.0464	DI 4	0.0069	0.0095
DC 1	0.0087	0.0147	DI 5	-0.0098	0.0098
DC 2	0.0018	0.0139	DI 6	-0.0055	0.0105
DC 3	-0.013	0.0143	DI 7	-0.017	0.0105
DC 4	0.0033	0.0145	DI 8	-0.047**	0.0168
DC 5	0.0027	0.0164	DI 9	-0.035*	0.0163
DC 6	0.550**	0.0325	DI10	-0.014	0.0227
D 1	-0.129**	0.0231	DI11	-0.044	0.0237
D 2	-0.232**	0.0197	DE 1	-0.027	0.0359
D 3	-0.254**	0.0493	DE 2	-0.022	0.0156
D 4	-0.252**	0.0227	DE 3	0.033	0.0197
D 5	-0.252**	0.0224	DE 4	-0.022	0.0156
D 6	-0.250**	0.0170	DE 5	0.077**	0.0229
D 7	-0.256**	0.0329	DE 6	-0.015	0.0106
D 8	-0.221**	0.0272	DE 7	-0.010	0.0088
D 9	-0.240**	0.0222	DE 8	-0.020	0.0217
D10	-0.257**	0.0493	DE 9	-0.029	0.0110
D11	-0.240**	0.0231	DE10	0.0036	0.0129
D12	-0.237**	0.0265	DE11	-0.011	0.0186
D13	-0.260**	0.0306	DE12	0.0061	0.0106
D14	-0.248**	0.0209	DE13	-0.011	0.0246
D15	-0.253**	0.0234	DE14	0.023	0.0126
D16	-0.243**	0.0180	DE15	-	-
D17	-0.221**	0.0234	DE16	0.060	0.0608
D18	-0.250**	0.0180	DE17	-	-
D19	-0.221**	0.0172	DH 1	-0.0072	0.0135
D20	-0.218**	0.0192	DH 2	-0.011	0.0110
D21	-0.221**	0.0172	DH 3	0.0076	0.0093
D22	-0.205**	0.0174	DH 4	0.034**	0.0121
D23	-0.164**	0.0185	DH 5	0.088**	0.0172

Constant 0.252

**   significant at 99%
*   significant at 95%

The following illustrates the main features of the regression:

Characteristic	Worker A		Worker B	
Sex	Male	0.0090	Male	0.0090
Age	Less than 25	0.0000	55-65	-0.0280
Social Class	Armed Forces	0.0550	Professional	0.0000
Industry	Public Admin. &		Wholesale &	
	Defence	-0.1640	Retail	-0.2210
Tenure	Over 5 years	0.0210	Over 5 years	0.0210
Income	£2000-£2500	0.0069	£2000-£2500	0.0069
Education	Apprenticeship	0.0061	HND	-0.0220
Hours worked	41-51	0.0340	31-41	0.0076
Constant of regression		0.2520		0.2520
Estimated Probability		0.7150		0.0255

Results from Townsend's Poverty Survey

The information collected in Professor P. Townsend's Survey of Household Resources and Standards of Living in the United Kingdom, 1968-9
was used to provide the empirical basis of his study on Poverty in
the United Kingdom (1979). The survey obtained information on a
range of fringe benefits, and in that sense this source is an improvement on the GHS. On the other hand its main disadvantage is that it
was conducted some 15 years ago, since when there has been a considerable growth of fringes. We believe, however, that it can still be
of some use in understanding the present situation, and of course it
remains ideal for an examination of a period of recent labour market
history.[3]

While much descriptive use was made of the fringe benefit data in
the published study, our aim was to investigate the major simultan-
eousdeterminants of fringes, based on a secondary analysis of the
data using multiple regression techniques. The raw sample of data
on employed workers contains a maximum of 2587 observations but, for
each regression we estimate a smaller sample is used, with the final
size in each case depending on the set of variables used and the
concomitant missing values. We were able to run regressions for sick
pay, pensions and lump-sum payments, holidays, company cars, meal
vouchers and subsidised meals. Table 5.5 gives the list of independent variables used, based on the same general considerations as
before but subject to their availability. Unlike with the GHS we had
no industry dummy, but a compensating gain was information on whether
respondents belonged to a union. Following the discussion of
Chapter 4 we expect unionisation to have an impact on holiday length
but have no strong expectations about its effect on other fringes.

Table 5.5   Independent Variables

Variable Label	Variable Name/Category
(i) Sex	
S1	Male Dummy Reference Category: Female
(ii) Age	Actual Age
(iii) Social Class	
C1	Semi-skilled Manuals Dummy
C2	Skilled Manuals Dummy
C3	Routine Non-manual Dummy
C4	Inspectional or Supervisory 'Lower' NM Dummy
C5	Inspectional or Supervisory 'Higher' NM Dummy
C6	Managerial & Executive Staffs Dummy
C7	Professionally Qualified & High Administration Reference Category: Unskilled Manuals
(iv) Wages	
WAGE	Weekly Wage (£ p.a.)
(v) Unionisation	
UNION	Union Membership Dummy Reference Category: Non-union Membership
(vi) Tenure	
TENURE	Over Five Years in Current Job Dummy Reference Category: Less than five years in current job.
(vii) Length of Working Week	
HOURS	Hours worked per week

(i)   Sickness Pay:

In order to examine this fringe, a linear probability model where the dependent variable (taking the values of zero or unity) is derived from responses to the question "are you entitled to sick pay from your employer?".   Table 5.6 presents the results.

It shows that 63.5 per cent of respondents who answered received sick pay from their employer.

Table 5.6   The Probability of Entitlement
                        to Sick Pay

Summary Statistics: $\overline{R}^2$ = 0.161, n = 2021, S = 0.44, Pr = 0.63, $F(13,2007)$ = 30.9 where Pr is the mean of dependent variable, in this case the relative frequency of sick pay entitlement.

Independent Variables

Label	Coefficient	Standard Error
WAGE	0.0021**	0.0007
AGE	0.0030**	0.0008
SEX	-0.0216	0.0243
C1	0.0857*	0.0410
C2	0.1540**	0.0378
C3	0.4308**	0.0456
C4	0.4355**	0.0453
C5	0.4767**	0.0458
C6	0.5225**	0.0631
C7	0.4234**	0.0655
TENURE	0.0704**	0.0223
UNION	0.0626**	0.0207
HOURS	0.0017**	0.0007
Constant	0.1228	

** significant at 99%
 * significant at 95%

While the $\overline{R}^2$ is rather low (0.161), the overall F-statistic is highly significant, as indeed are many of the individual t-statistics in the regression.   As we expected, tenure, wages, union membership, age and class all exert a direct effect on the probability of receiving sick pay.   Moreover, those working on a part-time basis have a lesser chance of receiving this fringe than those working a standard or longer week.   The sex dummy coefficient carries a negative sign but it is not significant at 95%.   On the whole these results confirm the findings of the GHS regression.   They suggest also that union membership is an additional significant variable raising the likelihood of receiving sick pay by about 6 percentage points.   We do not interpret this as necessarily implying that trade unions successfully pressed for better sick pay, for the effect is possibly indirect.   It could be that it indicates the increased likelihood of the individual being in an internal labour market, where fringes tend to be high.

But the main observation is the importance of social class.   The table suggests for example that an unskilled worker is by 0.52 less likely to be entitled to sick pay than a manager or executive. This, in view of the results from the General Household Survey, may be an over-estimate but it nevertheless indicates the presence of a significant inequality.

(ii)   Pensions and Lump-Sum Gratuities:
We used the same model to investigate the probability of receiving a pension.   Table 5.7 shows that of 1954 respondents to the questions "Will you receive a pension from your employer, if you stay in the job until retirement?", 51.6% said "yes".   The regression coeffic- ients confirm the importance of high class, long tenure, high income, and being male reported earlier in relation to the GHS findings. Unlike the latter, however, in this instance the length of the work- ing week and age though predictably signed are not significant. Moreover, membership of a trade union seems to improve ones chances of belonging to a private pension scheme by some 22 percentage points.   But since only a minority of unions were negotiating at that time over pensions we believe again that much of this effect is indirect.

Table 5.7   The Probability of Receiving a Pension

Summary Statistics: $\bar{R}^2$ = 0.24, n = 1954, F(13,1940) = 48.2, S = 0.44, Pr = 0.516

Independent Variables

Label	Coefficient	Standard Error
WAGE	0.0031**	0.0007
AGE	0.0003	0.0008
SEX	0.1279**	0.0244
C1	0.1748**	0.0409
C2	0.1569**	0.0378
C3	0.4128**	0.0461
C4	0.4601**	0.0453
C5	0.5142**	0.0460
C6	0.5696**	0.0641
C7	0.4463**	0.6949
TENURE	0.1195**	0.0223
UNION	0.2240**	0.0207
HOURS	0.0004	0.0007
Constant	-0.0906	

** significant at 99%
 * significant at 95%

It is noteworthy that in accordance with the GHS results, sex is significant in explaining pensions but not significant when explain- ing sick pay.   Finally, the statistical significance and quantita- tive importance of class both in this case and in the case of sick pay seem to support the view that the distinction between manual and non-manual employees is central in explaining the inequality in the distribution of certain fringe benefits.

We also examined, using standard regression models (not shown here) the determinants of the proportions of final salary paid out as a pension or as a lump sum. Confining the sample to those who were members of pension schemes, we found that, although income was insignificant, those in a higher social class had much better expectations. For example, being in the Professional and Higher Administration class meant that ceteris paribus one could expect an annual pension that as a ratio to final salary was 22 percentage points higher than that received by someone in the unskilled manual class.

Similarly, the lump sum would be 63 percentage points higher. A further finding was that males could expect a pension about 5 percentage points above that of females. These findings must be treated with some caution, in that quite a number of individuals did not respond to the relevant questions. Having said that, the factors which explain the distribution of pension scheme membership are to some extent reinforced by similar factors explaining the value of membership.

(iii)   Company Cars:
In our sample of 2100 employees used for regression estimation only 5.1 per cent enjoyed private use of a company car. The regression reported in Table 5.8 suggests that this privileged minority consisted mainly of men, of those who work longer hours and of those in higher social classes, i.e. professionals, managers, executives etc. Wages, age and tenure do not seem to be significant factors in this context, while being a member of a trade union tended to reduce one's chances of receiving this benefit.

The explanatory power of the regression, although statistically significant, is very low, suggesting that relevant variables are left out of the relationship used - the nature of the occupation as well as the size of business establishment are the most obvious ones.[4]

Table 5.8   The Probability of Having Free
                                Private Use of a Company Car

Summary Statistics: $\overline{R}^2$ = 0.07, n = 2100, F(13,2086) = 13.6,
                             S = 0.213, Pr = 0.051.

Independent Variables

Label	Coefficient	Standard Error
WAGE	0.00024	0.0004
AGE	-0.00034	0.0004
SEX	0.0539**	0.0114
C1	-0.0114	0.019
C2	0.0107	0.018
C3	0.0078	0.022
C4	0.0251	0.021
C5	0.1026**	0.022
C6	0.1169**	0.030
C7	0.1904**	0.031
TENURE	0.0078	0.011
UNION	-0.0453**	0.010
HOURS	0.0014**	0.0003
Constant	-0.0400	

** Significant at 99%
 * Significant at 95%

(iv)   Holidays:
The dependent variable in this case is the number of weeks paid holiday times the ratio of earnings per holiday-week over earnings per
working week.   This provides a measure of the value of this fringe
in relation to earnings.   Our estimated regressions are based on a
sample confined to those cases of no more than ten weeks holiday
entitlement.   This covers the overwhelming majority of the working
force and, in addition, it avoids the need for an interpretation of
the exceptional cases of a longer holiday entitlement.

Table 5.9 reports an estimate of the main influences.   It can be seen
that the holiday entitlement is higher for older, female, higher-paid
and long-tenured workers.   It also tends to be higher for workers
that belong to a trade-union and for non-manual than manual workers.
These results conform well with our expectations.   The only exception
is the finding that women enjoy more holidays than men.   Casual
observation suggests that this was not so, even in 1969 and we have
been unable to find an adequate specific explanation for this anomaly.

Table 5.9   Number of Weeks of Paid Holidays
                 Adjusted for Earnings (HOL)+

Summary Statistics: $\overline{R}^2$ = 0.206, n = 1953, F(13,1939) = 39.8,
                     S = 1.22

HOL(mean) = 2.05

Independent Variables

Label	Coefficient	Standard Error
WAGE	0.0101**	0.002
AGE	0.0112**	0.002
SEX	-0.2345**	0.069
C1	0.0539	0.114
C2	0.1932	0.105
C3	0.6856**	0.127
C4	1.1384**	0.126
C5	1.2776**	0.133
C6	1.3073**	0.197
C7	1.5952**	0.188
TENURE	0.2129**	0.063
HOURS	0.0020	0.002
UNION	0.2460**	0.058
Constant	0.8319	

+ Number of weeks times weekly earnings during the holiday period
   over weekly earnings while in work
** Significant at 99%

(v)   Subsidised Meals and Meal Vouchers:
About 26% of the respondents received subsidised meals.   Regression
analysis based on the Linear Probability Model showed that the likelihood of this benefit was higher for female unionised, high income and
high social class employees.   A further regression analysis showed
that the value of the subsidy - either in absolute terms or as a percentage of wages - tended to be higher for full-time, non-manual,
female and non-unionised employees.

Meal vouchers were received by a much lower proportion - only 3½%.
They were concentrated among non-manual, non-unionised younger and
long-tenured workers.   A regression using a sample confined to this
3½% showed that higher valued vouchers were received for those non-
unionised, young male workers with higher wages.   However a considerable amount of the variation of these subsidies and vouchers is not
explained by our regressions and we suspect that the nature of the
occupation, the type of industry and the size of establishment may be
important additional factors not included in our regression.

(vi)   Other Fringes:
The Survey provides information on a number of other fringe benefits
including benefits-in-kind, cheap goods, medical expenses and travel
costs.   With the exception of free or cheap goods that were received
by about 22% of the employees in the sample, the rest of the fringe

71

benefits in this category were only available to between 0.3 and 3.9 per cent of the employees. Females, unskilled manual workers, trade unionists and part-time workers were less likely to receive benefits-in-kind. When all these 'other' fringes are considered together those workers who are male, who earn high incomes, work long hours, are not manual, are not members of a trade union and have a long tenure, tend to benefit more than the rest.

Summary

The foregoing suggests that most of the independent variables considered contribute significantly to an explanation of both the incidence and the relative importance of fringe benefits. There remains some scope for improving the explanatory power of the estimated relationships. One important variable - size of establishment - was not available with either data source and hence was excluded. Nonetheless some of the results are robust in the sense that the estimated coefficients remain highly significant under alternative specifications and that, where possible, they are confirmed by both data sets. In the second part of the next chapter we summarise these conclusions along with those from our industry-level analysis, and draw out the empirical and theoretical implications regarding the distribution of fringes. At this stage we merely list very briefly our main results so far, by way of taking stock:

   (i)   The major fringes are positively influenced by income

  (ii)   Long job-tenure increases the likelihood of receiving pensions, sick pay and holidays, but not in the case of high income earners.

 (iii)   Fringes improve with occupational class status, with a particularly sharp difference between those of manual and non-manual workers.

  (iv)   Being full-time as opposed to part-time improves the chances of receiving many fringes.

   (v)   Being male improves the chance of receiving a pension compared to being female, but it makes no difference in regard to sick pay.

  (vi)   As we suspected, age does have an effect: being older at least up till the age of 55, improves the chances of belonging to a sick pay scheme, of receiving a longer holiday and probably of belonging to a pension scheme.

 (vii)   Some industry dummy variables are significant determinants, indicating the existence of factors not captured by other variables.

Footnotes

1. Regressions were run with alternative measures of educational
    attainment and social class. The Hope-Goldthorpe Value was
    used for the latter variable and the Age-left-school for the
    former. The results obtained under this alternative were, on
    the whole, worse in terms of coefficients, t-statistics and R^2,
    than the ones already reported.

2. When the alternative measures of education and social class were
    used (see note 1) the overall results are not improved. The
    Hope-Goldthorpe variable is not significant while the Age-left-
    school variable does suggest that staying in school longer
    improves one's chances of belonging to a pension scheme.

3. See Townsend (1979), Ch. 3, for details on the methods used in
    carrying out the Survey.

4. The results in the text are confirmed by regressions that explain
    both the absolute value of this benefit and the value as a per-
    centage of wages. In both cases, however, the explanatory
    power of the regression is low. (On the basis of the sample
    used the average value of the company car benefits for those who
    enjoy it represents about six per cent of the annual wage.)

CHAPTER 6

THE DISTRIBUTION OF FRINGES: II

In this chapter we have two objectives. First we make use of a
rich data source, a survey of industrial labour costs, to supplement
and, hopefully, confirm the results reported in the last chapter.
Second we summarise our overall conclusions based on both individual
and industry-level analyses, regarding what factors determine the
distribution of fringe benefits in Britain.

Results from the 1978 Labour Cost Survey
This survey of businesses, which is carried out every three years by
the Department of Employment, contains information on the costs to
employers of most fringe benefits. The results are tabulated and
published on an industry basis and we were able to work partly with
these published tables in chapter 2. Here we mainly used some unpublished, less aggregated tables made available to us.[1]

Two series were used. Series A took the form of values of various
fringe benefit components of labour costs per hour, by industry
order by size of establishment, for manual and non-manual workers
separately. This gave us a maximum of 200 observations, 100 each
for manuals and non-manuals, obtained as follows: for sixteen
production industries there were six size ranges each, while for four
production industries no size ranges were specified.[2] Series B took
the form of values of fringe benefit costs per hour by Minimum List
Heading (MLH) industry. This gave a maximum of 122 observations.
This series while being at a more disaggregated industry level was
not broken down by size or by type of worker.

Compared to our data sources used in the previous chapter, these
series have the advantage of being much more comprehensive: they
cover a wider range of benefits, and they give some measure of the
values of fringes to employees beyond the extent of their coverage -
even if the cost to the employer somewhat understates, in the case
of fringes subject to tax exemption, the value to the employee.
Moreover, a possibly important variable, available here but not included in Chapter 5, was size of establishment. The fringes listed
are 'Voluntary Social Welfare Payments','Benefits in Kind' and 'Subsidised Services' (see Chapter 2 for definitions). Unfortunately
the costs of company cars are (surprisingly) not counted as part of
labour costs, and nor were holiday costs available.

The disadvantage of these series is that they are of course at the industry level. This requires us to consider how far the factors which we think are important in explaining individuals' fringes will show up on our data.

On the basis of our arguments in Chapters 3 and 4 we expect that the fringe shares - particularly the tenure-related fringes such as pensions (which come under Voluntary Social Welfare Payments) - should increase with the size and non-manual worker dummies. With other variables we use as independent variable the average value for each unit. Thus we hypothesise that fringe shares rise with the average wage, the average tenure and the degree of unionisation, but fall with the ratios of female and part-time workers. (Additionally, we experimented also with average size and proportions of non-manual workers in place of dummy variables.) These hypotheses are based on the plausible assumption that what is true for most individuals will be reflected in the averages for each observation unit, but it should be noted that this could be faulty. Within each industry, and indeed within each firm, there may be a mixture of primary and secondary labour markets, which could conceivably upset the assumption.

In working with these series we introduced two further possible indices of their structure. First, we introduced the variability of output as a regressor, (rather unsuccessfully as it turned out). The larger it is, the greater ceteris paribus will be the variation in the demand for labour, and hence the more likely it is that firms will go for a secondary labour market strategy. It is of course possible that a firm operating in a primary sector, 'core', product market could rely heavily on a secondary labour market (Lawson, 1981), but we think this relatively uncommon, and confined mainly to paternalistic firms. Accordingly, we hypothesised a negative relationship between output variability and fringe share.

Second, we tested for the effect of unemployment. Theoretically, this has an uncertain effect on the share of fringes. On the one hand it provides another measure of the prevalence of internal labour markets in the industry. For in a recession it is generally secondary workers who lose their jobs first. In the course of a full cycle, average unemployment is lower in the primary labour markets. On the other hand for the self-same reason unemployment in an industry would eliminate disproportionately those with lower fringe shares, leaving the high fringe workers behind.

We examined the various hypotheses using a standard linear multiple regression analysis, where the dependent variable was in turn each of the three types of fringe as a proportion of wages and salaries. A full list of independent variables is given in Table 6.1. Of these, only 'turnover' requires further explanation: this was used as an alternative to our tenure variable, both as a check and as an alternative in those cases where tenure could not be used (at the MLH level). We assumed that tenure was strongly negatively correlated with turnover.[3]

Table 6.1   Definition of Variables

1. Dependent Variables

RVSWP   = ratio of voluntary social welfare payments to wages,%.
RBIK   = ratio of benefits in kind to wages, %.
RSS   = ratio of subsidised services to wages, %.
RFB   = RVSWP + RBIK + RSS

2. Independent Variables

WAGE   = wage level, pence per hour[**]
NONMAN   = type of worker dummy; non-manual = 1, 0 otherwise
NONMANRAT = ratio of non-manual to total employees (MLH level), %.
SIZE   = establishment size, average number of employees per
              establishment
S2-S6   = establishment size dummies; for size specification see
              Appendix I
VOUTPUT   = variability of output[*]
FEMALE   = proportion of female workers, %.
FPTIME   = proportion of female part-time workers, %.
p-TIME   = proportion of part-time workers, %.
TUDENS   = trade union density, %.
UNEMP   = unemployment rate, %.
TENURE   = proportion of workers with a tenure of over 10 years,%.
TURNOVER   = turnover,[*] % per 4 weeks.

                (IND1 = Paper, Printing and Publishing
                (IND2 = Timber and Furniture
                (IND3 = Bricks, Pottery, Glass, Cement, etc.
                (IND4 = Clothing and Footwear
                (IND5 = Leather, Leather Goods and Fur
                (IND6 = Textiles
                (IND7 = Other Metal Goods
[***]   (IND8 = Vehicles
Industry   (IND9 = Shipbuilding and Marine Engineering
Dummies   (IND10 = Electrical Engineering
(SIC, 1968)   (IND11 = Instrument Engineering
                (IND12 = Mechanical Engineering
                (IND13 = Metal Manufacture
                (IND14 = Chemical and Allied Industries
                (IND15 = Food, Drink and Tobacco
                (IND16 = Coal and Petroleum Products
                (IND17 = Construction
                (IND18 = Gas, Electricity and Water
                (IND19 = Mining and Quarrying

RC (Reference Category) - Other Manufacturing Industries

---

*   See Appendix
**   The wage variable stands for wages and salaries and includes all
     overtime, bonuses etc., gross of tax, national insurance etc.
     The hours used as denominator for a number of variables included
     overtime, but excluded sickness time off, mealtime and holiday
     time-off.
*** Coverage differs slightly from Chapter 5; hence the coding of
     dummies is different.

For a number of potential regressors, data by size of establishment
are not available. These include tenure, turnover, trade union
density, the rate of unemployment, the proportion of female workers,
the proportion of part-time female workers, and the variability of
output. For each of these variables we have only one observation
per industry, which is therefore used for all six size ranges.
Furthermore, for some of these variables data are not available for
all production industries (e.g. turnover is only available for manufacturing industries) and not all variables are available at MLH
level (e.g. trade union density, variability of output). Our
response to these various problems with the data was to run a number
of regressions varying the sample used and the regressors included
in order to check for the robustness of our results. Thus, apart
from using the full samples, in some cases we excluded the non-manufacturing industries, in others we excluded industries with a single
size range, and we also examined the samples for manual and non-
manual workers separately.[4]

(i)   Voluntary Social Welfare Payments (VSWP):
Tables 6.2 and 6.3 show results based on Series A and B respectively.

Table 6.2 confirms our expectation that VSWP, as a ratio to wages,
is considerably greater for non-manual workers. It also increases
with the size of establishment and with the proportion of tenured
workers in the industry. For example, establishments with over
1000 employees are estimated to have, ceteris paribus, a ratio of
VSWP to wages some 3.7 percentage points above that for establishments with less than 50 employees. The wage coefficient is positive,
as expected, but not significant at the 95% level. The coefficient
on variability of output is, surprisingly, positive, but it is also
insignificant. Other variables which when introduced were very insignificant were the proportion of females, trade union density, and
the level of unemployment. However, an unexpected result is that
the coefficient on the proportion of part-time female workers is
positive and significant. We find this anomaly difficult to ration-
alise, in view of the opposite effect suggested by our individual
cross-section results of last chapter. Part of the explanation may
be that here we are examining industry-level data, which as suggested
above need not necessarily always give the same results as for
individuals due to the coexistence of different types of labour
markets within each industry. In addition, it should be remembered
the data for this variable were not broken down by size range.

In Table 6.3 we see that the significance of establishment size is
confirmed at MLH level, and that, as expected, a higher turnover
(which is our proxy for lower tenure) is associated with a lower
ratio of VSWP. In addition, average wages and the proportion of
non-manual workers are correctly signed but not quite significant.
In the case of the latter, we believe that the availability of
separate data for manual and non-manual workers as in Series A gave
the more reliable result. The table also shows that the unemployment coefficient was positive though insignificant. Other variables

which when introduced were very insignificant were the proportions of female and part-time workers.

Table 6.2   <u>Regression with Voluntary Social</u>
<u>Welfare Payments as % of Wages</u>
<u>as Dependent Variable (Series A)</u>

<u>Summary Statistics:</u> $\overline{R}^2$ = 0.887, n = 160, F(17,142) = 74.1
Standard Error = 1.20, $\overline{Y}$ = 5.82 (Mean of
Dependent
Variable)

Independent Variables:

	Label	Coefficient	Standard Error
	(WAGE	0.0074	0.007
Mainstream	(NONMAN	4.58**	0.452
Economic	(FPTIME	0.18**	0.035
Variables	(TENURE	0.042**	0.012
	(VOUTPUT	16.62	10.394
	(S2	1.20**	0.334
	(S3	1.93**	0.340
Size	(S4	2.40**	0.349
Dummies	(S5	2.94**	0.376
	(S6	3.73**	0.473
	(IND3	0.76	0.408
	(IND4	-1.92**	0.519
	(IND13	1.59**	0.404
Industry	(IND14	2.80**	0.438
Dummies	(IND15	1.35*	0.520
	(IND18	6.58**	0.960
	(IND19	4.75	2.469

Constant -4.96

*   Significant at 95%
**   Significant at 99%

These results were elaborated in a number of ways by running further regressions with different independent variables and sample sizes. For example in series B we expanded the sample to include non-manufacturing industries. This led to a significant positive coefficient on wages and a nagative coefficient for part-time workers; but turnover had to be excluded for lack of availability. In series A, we used the whole sample of 200 observations. This meant excluding tenure, but the substantive conclusions of Table 6.2 were not altered. Another variation was to use turnover instead of tenure in series A. Again, the main economic variables retained their significance, while turnover had a negative sign. A further experiment with series A was to replace the size dummies with 'SIZE', the average size of establishment. The coefficient was significantly positive, and meanwhile the wage coefficient became positive and significant, other results not changing much.

78

Table 6.3   Regression with Voluntary Social
                      Welfare Payments as % of Wages
                      as Dependent Variable (Series B)

Summary Statistics: $\overline{R}^2$ = 0.771, n = 116, $F(15,100)$ = 26.8
                       Standard Error = 1.42, $\overline{Y}$ = 5.48 (Mean of
                                                 Dependent
                                                 Variable)

Independent Variables:

	Label	Coefficient	Standard Error
Mainstream	(WAGE	0.0088	0.009
Economic	(SIZE	0.021**	0.001
Variables	(NONMANRAT	0.040	0.024
	(UNEMP	22.53	12.184
	(TURNOVER	-0.63**	0.170
	(IND2	-0.82	0.643
	(IND4	-1.62*	0.658
	(IND5	-2.39*	0.959
	(IND6	-1.08*	0.518
Industry	(IND10	-1.76**	0.570
Dummies	(IND11	1.67*	0.756
	(IND13	1.02	0.652
	(IND14	2.58**	0.570
	(IND15	1.56**	0.473
	(IND16	8.98**	1.105

Constant 3.65

*   Significant at 95%
** Significant at 99%

In these variations the industries included in the sample also change,
but there was a recurrent pattern of significant dummy coefficient
estimates, indicating that not all of the variation has been explained
by our economic variables and that some of it is due to the specific
traditions of different industries. The recurrent pattern of these
coefficients, indicates that Coal and Petroleum products, Mining and
Quarrying and Gas, Electricity and Water are high fringe benefits
industries. Other industries associated with positive and significant coefficients are Chemicals and Allied industries, Metal Manufacture, and Food, Drink and Tobacco. On the other hand VSWP seem
to be relatively low in Clothing and Footwear and in Electrical
Engineering. These observations are consistent with our findings
for pensions and sick pay from the General Household Survey in Chapter 5. Two of the consistently high VSWP industries (Mining and
Quarrying and Gas, Electricity and Water) are traditional public
sector industries with high trade union density while Clothing and
Footwear, an industry consistently associated with low fringe benefits, is characterised by a high variability in output and employment,
with dominant secondary labour market conditions.

(ii) Benefits-in-Kind:
At only 0.31% of average wages in the production industries, benefits-in-kind are not very important quantitatively.   Moreover, this
average would have been smaller still but for two extreme industries:
Mining and Quarrying (4.62%) and Coal and Petroleum (1.43%).   Tables
6.4 and 6.5 report two illustrative regression analyses based on
series A and B respectively.

In series A, the ratio of Benefits-in-Kind to wages was higher for
non-manual workers and in industries with a high proportion of
tenured workers.   The coefficients on the proportion of female
workers, and the medium size dummies were negative but not particularly significant.   Meanwhile (not shown) the other size dummies,
wages and all other mainstream economic variables had a negligible
impact.   When turnover was used instead of tenure, this too was insignificant.   The lack of explanatory power was mirrored in the
series B results, but there we did find a negative coefficient on
unemployment.   Surprisingly we also found a small but significant
negative impact from the proportion of non-manual workers, which is
inconsistent with the series A conclusion based on dummy variables
(which we consider more plausible).

Table 6.4   Regression with Benefits-in-Kind
                 as % of Wages as Dependent
                 Variable (Series A)

Summary Statistics: $\overline{R}^2$ = 0.707, n = 160, F(11,148) = 35.9
                     Standard Error = 0.22, $\overline{Y}$ = 0.18 (Mean of
                                                                   Dependent
                                                                   Variable)

Independent Variables:

	Label	Coefficient	Standard Error
Mainstream Economic Variables	(WAGE		
	(NONMAN	0.12**	0.038
	(FEMALE	−0.0031	0.002
	(TENURE	0.0045*	0.002
Size Dummies	(S3	−0.050	0.048
	(S4	−0.063	0.048
Industry Dummies	(IND4	0.18	0.094
	(IND8	−0.13	0.079
	(IND9	−0.081	0.071
	(IND15	0.25**	0.070
	(IND18	−0.23	0.102
	(IND19	2.88**	0.168

                 Constant -0.13

*   Significant at 95%
**   Significant at 99%

On the whole it is apparent that the most important determinant of
the distribution of benefits in kind are the nature and line of

production of an establishment or industry. A case in question is
the Mining and Quarrying Industry in which the provision of free coal
raises the benefits in kind ratio to an exceptionally high level.
Also significant are the Food, Drink and Tobacco and the Coal and
Petroleum Products industries. It is noticeable the products of
all these can be consumer goods, and hence are more likely to be
demanded by workers than in some others where the products are only
usable as intermediate goods.

Table 6.5   Regression with Benefits-in-Kind
                   as % of Wages as Dependent
                   Variable (Series B)

Summary Statistics: $\overline{R}^2$ = 0.697, n = 122, F(7,114) = 40.8
                      Standard Error = 0.34, $\overline{Y}$ = 0.18 (Mean of
                                                         Dependent
                                                         Variable)

Independent Variables:

	Label	Coefficient	Standard Error
Mainstream	(NONMANRAT	-0.0081*	0.004
Economic	(P-TIME	-0.0047	0.006
Variables	(UNEMP	-4.81*	2.402
	(IND14	0.16	0.127
Industry	(IND15	0.25*	0.100
Dummies	(IND16	2.37**	0.250
	(IND19	4.66**	0.359

Constant 0.54

*   Significant at 95%
** Significant at 99%

(iii) Subsidised Services:
The third category of fringes we look at here is subsidised services.
For all production industries these cost on a (weighted) average 1.61
per cent of the wage level.   They are the least variable of the
types of fringe benefits we consider, (as may be seen at a glance
from Table 2.13).

The regression estimated on the basis of the full sample of series A
is reported in Table 6.6.   The results suggest that provision of
this benefit relative to wages increases with the level of wages and
is greater for industries with a higher percentage of female part-
time employees.   Furthermore, it is higher for manual than non-
manual workers, but lower for industries with a relatively high unemployment.   The size dummy coefficients are all significant and
suggest that the fringe share of this type increases with size.
There are several significant industry dummies.   On the negative
side are industries like Paper, Printing and Publishing, Textiles,
Shipbuilding and Marine Engineering.   On the positive side, being in
the Mining and Quarrying, Coal and Petroleum Products or Food, Drink
and Tobacco industries raises the level of subsidised services on
average.

81

Table 6.6   Regression with Subsidised Services
as % Wages as Dependent
Variable (Series A)

Summary Statistics: $\overline{R}^2$ = 0.729, n = 200, F(23,176) = 24.3
Standard Error = 0.38, $\overline{Y}$ = 1.45 (Mean of
Dependent
Variable)

Independent Variables:

	Label	Coefficient	Standard Error
Mainstream	(WAGE	0.0025	0.002
Economic	(NONMAN	-0.29*	0.140
Variables	(FPTIME	0.021	0.011
	(UNEMP	-6.91**	1.473
	(S2	0.45**	0.097
Size	(S3	0.69**	0.099
Dummies	(S4	0.96**	0.102
	(S5	1.14**	0.112
	(S6	0.89**	0.139
	(IND1	-0.36**	0.131
	(IND2	-0.19	0.122
	(IND3	0.18	0.122
	(IND4	-0.29	0.162
	(IND5	0.29	0.287
Industry	(IND6	-0.27*	0.130
Dummies	(IND7	0.13	0.124
	(IND9	-0.33**	0.123
	(IND11	-0.16	0.131
	(IND14	0.79**	0.133
	(IND15	0.56**	0.144
	(IND16	2.08**	0.320
	(IND18	-0.45	0.296
	(IND19	2.65**	0.327

Constant 0.54

*   Significant at 95%
**   Signiciant at 99%

These latter high dummy coefficients are confirmed in a regression
based on series B, shown in Table 6.7.   This indicates also a significantly positive effect for wages and negative effect for the proportion of part-time workers, as expected.   Other independent economic variables were not significant, including the proportion of non-
manual workers and turnover.   The former result differs from series
A, but the latter confirms the finding we obtained from experimenting
with different samples and variables using series A: tenure and turnover were insignificant.   Trade union density had no impact, and
variability of output had no consistent effect.   There was a tendency in some cases for the coefficient on the proportion of female
workers to be negative and significant, 6.7.

Table 6.7   Subsidised Services - All Variables Specified

Summary Statistics: R^2 = 0.522, n = 116, $F(17,98)$ = 8.4
Standard Error = 0.50, $\bar{Y}$ = 1.66 (Mean of Dependent Variable)

Independent Variables:

	Label	Coefficients	Standard Error
Mainstream Economic Variables	(WAGE	0.0062*	0.003
	(SIZE	0.00045	0.000
	(FEMALE	0.010	0.006
	(P-TIME	-0.034*	0.016
	(UNEMP	-0.057	3.922
	(TURNOVER	0.094	0.060
Industry Dummies	(IND1	-0.28	0.229
	(IND2	-0.52*	0.241
	(IND3	0.25	0.244
	(IND4	-0.43	0.283
	(IND6	-0.26	0.181
	(IND7	0.15	0.199
	(IND8	-0.58*	0.256
	(IND11	-0.44	0.273
	(IND14	0.51*	0.200
	(IND15	0.66**	0.174
	(IND16	1.70**	0.381

Constant 0.13

*   Significant at 95%
**   Significant at 99%

Summary and Conclusion: The Factors Explaining the Distribution of Fringes

In Chapter 2 we documented the known facts about the distribution of many types of fringe benefit. It was clear that several fringes were very unequally distributed amongst people, in that the ratio of the fringe value to wages was positively correlated with income. However, we also saw that this ratio depended too on a number of other factors, suggested either by our theory or by observation or by previous studies of the US labour market. In this chapter and the previous one we have used multiple regression techniques to try to disentangle the various major factors in the British labour market. We were to a considerable extent successful in this, though in a number of cases the summary statistics suggest that a good deal of the variation remains unexplained. Our main conclusions are robust in that certain determinants were shown to be important under a variety of different specifications and using different data sets.[8] We now summarise the implications of our results, taking in turn each of the main factors discussed in Chapter 4.

(1)   Wages:
We can confirm that, in Britain, there is a small positive effect of
wages on the fringe benefit share.   Our estimates were that a rise
of 10 pence an hour in wages (about 5% of the national average)
would lead to a rise in the ratio of Voluntary Social Welfare Payments to wages (RVSWP) by 0.07 percentage points, a rise of between
.02 and .06 percentage points in the ratio of Subsidised Services to
wages (RSS) and no effect on the Benefits-in-Kind ratio (RBIK).
According to the Townsend survey, a £1 a week rise in income (about
5% of average income at the time) led to a 0.3 and 0.2 percentage
point rise in the probability of having pensions and sick pay rights,
and a very small increase in holiday length.   While other specifications suggest that the effect may be a bit larger, the overriding
impression is that they are not very high compared to the impact of
other factors.

Our evidence does not allow us to distinguish between the various
theoretical causes of this effect.   It could be due to a tax effect,
an income elasticity of demand greater than one, or an indirect
effect associated with the structuring of labour markets.   In any
case, none of these seems to be especially strong.

(ii) Tenure:
Our evidence strongly confirms the proposition that certain fringe
benefits are tenure-related.   For example, our GHS estimates are
that the employee with over five years' job tenure, compared to one
with between three and twelve months, was 20 percentage points more
likely to receive sick pay and 24 percentage points more likely to
be expecting a pension.   Meanwhile a 10% rise in the proportions
having over 10 years job-tenure in an industry raises RVSWP by about
0.4 percentage points.   However, it must be noted that in the case
of this factor a 2-way causation may exist: not only does high
tenure mean high fringes, also fringes are designed to induce high
tenure by penalising quitters.   Our coefficients reflect the combination of these two effects.

We also found that tenure was not a significant determinant for high
income earners.   This is consistent with our argument that, for
them, fringes are not used as a device for maintaining internal
labour markets - because it was worthwhile for job applicants to gain
full information about them (see Chapter 3).

Finally, with other fringes the evidence suggests no effect or
possibly a small one (in the case of benefits in kind).   In other
words, things like subsidised canteens, medical services and so on,
are made available immediately to new employees.

(iii) Size:
The evidence from our industry analysis is strongly that size has a
big effect on some fringes.   For example, being in a 500 to 1,000
employee establishment, compared with one with 10 to 49 employees,
raises RVSWP by nearly 3 percentage points (while the national

average is 5.8%), and RSS by over 1.1 percentage points (national average 1.5%). There was a negligible effect on benefits in kind.

These estimates reflect both the economies of scale in provision of fringes and also, particularly for the pensions and sick pay fringes of VSWP, the greater prevalence of internal labour markets in large firms and establishments.

(iv) Type of Worker:
(a) Class: Again, we can be unequivocal that being of higher occupational status has a large effect on fringes. In fact, it is generally the most important single influence. There is a particularly sharp distinction between non-manual and manual workers' fringes. For example, we estimated from the GHS that the junior non-manual, compared to the skilled manual worker, was (ceteris paribus) 13 percentage points more likely to expect a pension and 24 percentage points more likely to have a right to sick pay. (The Townsend survey equivalent figures were 24 and 28 percentage points respectively.) This was consistent with our other estimates, that being non-manual raised Voluntary Social Welfare Payments over wages (RVSWP) on average by over 4 percentage points, compared to being manual.

With benefits in kind the evidence is less overwhelming but still strong. Series A estimates put the effect at 0.12 percentage points (compared to a national average for RBIK of 0.18%). Series B estimates, which are less sound in this case, failed to confirm this, but estimates from Townsend were consistent with a positive effect. Meanwhile the effect on subsidised services is estimated to be quite small and the evidence from different sources is conflicting.

These results show that, as far as the major fringes are concerned, manual workers are trebly disadvantaged. Their fringes are in absolute terms low, and in addition they are relatively low as a proportion to their wages because their wages are themselves low. But, what is much more important, their fringe benefit ratio is low because they are manual workers. In other words, we have here confirmed the hypothesis of Townsend (1979) and others that manual workers are singled out for poor treatment (a hypothesis that remained unproven until the impact of all relevant factors could be simultaneously taken into account). Pension and sick pay arrangements tend to be complex and opaque, and this might explain why there is an especially strong effect for these types of fringes. According to Townsend's hypothesis, employers make use of the lack of information to obscure larger differentials. However, this would require further research to be substantiated - our findings are equally consistent with the theoretical arguments for the segmentation of labour markets. Moreover it is clear also from our analysis (as well as from Table 2.18) that company cars, which are fairly visible, are also very strongly determined by occupational status seeming thus to advertise the disparities in remuneration.

(b) Full-time/Part-time: There is some evidence that full-timers
do better than part-timers.

With regard to subsidised services, Series B estimates implied part-
timers are worse off, and this is consistent with our individual
estimates that part-timers received (ceteris paribus) less subsidised
meals. Other results are somewhat conflicting. For example, GHS
estimates were that working full time (31 to 41 hours per week) compared to part time (11 to 21 hours) raised the likelihood of getting
sick pay and pensions by 16 and 26 percentage points respectively.
The Townsend survey confirmed a small effect, but the industry-level
estimates failed to confirm this, even suggesting a positive relation
between the proportion of female part-timers and the ratio of voluntary social welfare payments to wages.

Despite these conflicting results we are inclined to take the GHS
estimates as more reliable, in that they are individual-based. But
further research would be necessary to substantiate this, and also to
examine how far it is due to the higher costs of administration for
part-timers and how far to the greater association of part-time work
with other secondary labour market characteristics.

(c) Female/Male: Our estimates show no effect of sex on the likelihood of getting sick pay, but that being male raises the chance of
expecting a pension by 8 or 13 percentage points according to our two
individual data sources. Meanwhile being female raises the chance
of getting subsidised meals, a result of which is weakly confirmed
by the Labour Cost analysis. However the latter found no significant evidence of any effect on the other fringes.

Again, given this conflicting evidence, we find the individual-based
results more convincing, but even they do not imply substantial
discrimination. Despite the fact that the percentage of non-manual
males with pension rights exceeds that for females by 21 points,
while with manuals the margin is 25 points, most of these differences
are accounted for by the other independent variables.

(v) Union Membership:
The individual-based estimates of Townsend showed that being in a
union raised the likelihood of getting sick pay and pension rights by
6 and 22 percentage points respectively but lowered the chances of
getting a company car by 5 points. None of these constitute evidence that unions consciously and successfully bargained for (or
against) such fringes (see Chapter 3). Moreover the estimates were
not confirmed at the industry level, where no effect of union density
could be discovered. However, given that unions have bargained over
holidays for a long time, it is interesting to note our estimate that
being a union member raised paid holidays by about a quarter of a
week in 1969 when the average holiday week was only just over two
weeks.[9]

(vi) Other Factors:
At the industry level unemployment had a negative effect on the benefits in kind and subsidised services ratios. This is consistent
with the idea that the variable is an index of the importance of
secondary labour markets in an industry, but the theoretical effect
is ambiguous and in any case no significant negative effect was found
in the case of voluntary social welfare payments.[9]

Finally it has been found that industry dummy variables contribute to
the explanation, suggesting there are certain characteristics not
picked up in our main economic variables. These may be qualitative
or difficult to observe, such as paternalism, tradition, nature of
product and so on. For example, there are it seems traditionally
high fringe industries (such as Mining and Quarrying; Gas, Electricity and Water; Chemical and Allied; Public Administration) and low
fringe industries (such as Clothing and Footwear, Textiles, Timber
and Furniture and so on).

To some extent we would explain the high fringe industries as due to
being in the public sector, though this applies mainly to the wel-
fare-type benefits.[10] Also it is known that firms in industries
such as Textiles tend to employ secondary labour market strategies.
This may not be fully captured by our other independent variables and
hence it is consistent with our theoretical approach that being in
this industry leads to low fringes.

In Sum:
Most of these results add to the gradually growing body of knowledge
about fringe benefits, and in particular they allow for the first
time a picture of the major factors at work which determine the distribution of fringes in British industry. These results are consistent with the theoretical arguments we reviewed in Chapter 3, as well
as being of interest in themselves. They also throw some light on
the question of the widespread growth of fringes, a subject to which
we now turn.

Footnotes

1. See Employment Gazette, Sept. 1980 and Jan. 1981. We are grateful to the Department of Employment for supplying extra tables. Unfortunately they were unable to provide us with data on holidays and other time-off with pay at a disaggregated level. This was due to cuts in the statistical service and the problem of maintaining confidentiality of respondents.

2. An exception is that the size ranges for Construction were on the basis of firms, not establishments. Exclusion of this industry does not substantially alter the results, and we pre-ferred to leave it in.

3. This assumption was validated in those samples where both vari-ables were available.

4. Once we had established a sound rationale for the specifications to be estimated, we carried out a forward stepwise estimation process within an SPSS package. According to this procedure the explanatory variables enter the regression one at a time until, in the last step, all the independent variables appear in the equation as regressors. In the course of this process when, after a particular step, newly included regressors (1) are not statistically significant, (ii) do not alter significantly the size of the other parameters and of the accompanied t-statistics, and (iii) do not lead to a rise in the adjusted R^2, we take that particular step-specification to be the optimal one and consider the excluded potential regressors as 'irrelevant' or 'super-fluous' variables (Rao and Miller, 1971, pp.35-37).

5. As a further variation we split series A into a manual and a non-manual set, and ran separate regressions. IN the case of man-ual workers the tenure and the size dummies are accompanied by coefficients which are both significant and bear the expected sign. The regression suggests that the fringe share tends to fall as the proportion of female workers increases, but the same anomolous result as before appears also: the proportion of female part-time employees seems to be positively related with the fringe share. In the case of non-manual workers, the size dummies and wages were significant, but the tenure coefficient was very insignificant.

6. Regressions run separately for manual and non-manual workers differ in a number of ways: for non-manuals the only significant regressors were wages, the size dummies and a few industry dummies; for manuals, the proportions of female and female part-time employees, unemployment and even turnover appear to be sign-ificant regressors. Wages do not appear to be significant.

7. As an additional experiment we ran regressions to explain
    aggregate fringes.   We treat these with some caution, since it
    is clear from other results that the independent variables have
    different effects on each type of fringe.   To summarise the
    findings: wages, tenure or turnover, proportion of part-time
    females, and occasionally trade union density all raise the
    proportion of aggregate fringes.   The overall results are in
    fact not very different from those for VSWP which is the major
    component.   See Green, Hadjimatheou and Smail (1984b) for
    details.

8. Although the available surveys are not as up to date as we would
    have wished, there is no reason to believe that the major hypo-
    theses will have changed substantially since 1978.   Results
    from the 1981 Labour Cost Survey were not made available until
    after our empirical work was completed.   The published tables
    do not suggest any major structural changes between 1978 and
    1981 that might undermine our conclusions.

9. The coefficient estimates of variability of output were quite
    unstable under specification changes, and we cannot therefore
    draw any implications.

10. According to an IDS Study (1983), the public sector also has a
    more ageing workforce than the rest of the economy.

Appendix: Definitions and Data Sources

1.   The size dummies (S2-S6) were specified as follows:

           S2 = 1 for   50   -   99 employees
           S3 = 1 for   100   -   199 employees
           S4 = 1 for   200   -   499 employees
           S5 = 1 for   500   -   999 employees
           S6 = 1 for 1000 +   employees
           S1 = 0 for   10   -   49 employees, reference category.

     As an alternative to this we occasionally used an estimate of
     the average size of establishment in each industry based on
     data from the CSO Annual Abstract (1982).

2.   The turnover variable was calculated as the sum of engagement
     rates and voluntary discharge rates per month; the data are
     obtained from the Employment Gazette.   The tenure variable was
     based on the figures given by Main (1982), not available at MLH
     level.   Unfortunately, the initial year for Main's long-term
     study was prior to 1968, when the current SIC was established.
     Thus a few newer industrial orders are omitted from our data
     set, reducing our sample size slightly when this variable was
     used.

3.   The rate of unemployment per industry was calculated from data
     in the Employment Gazette and from the Census of Production for
     October 1978.   The latter source provides the data on which the
     variability of output estimate was based: this is measured by
     the standard error of the linear time-trend regression for out-
     put in 1969-1978.   Also from this source we obtained the pro-
     portions of female workers, part-time workers and non-manual
     workers in each MLH industry, as well as the average size of
     establishments.

4.   Average wage levels were supplied with the Labour Cost Survey
     data.

CHAPTER 7

THE GROWTH OF FRINGES

Introduction

In Chapter 2 the basic facts about the tremendous growth of fringe
benefits over the last two decades were outlined.   However, unlike
with the distribution question, this growth is not easily amenable
to formal statistical analysis, since we do not have adequate time
series data.

To some extent, the conclusions of the cross-section analysis may be
applied to formulate hypotheses about the growth of fringes, but
this remains an inexact method.   Over time, preferences and attitudes may change, and moreover our cross-section results made no
allowance for time series factors, (such as the stage of the business cycle).   Nonetheless these results do serve as useful pointers
to the more important factors, provided no attempt is made to measure
too precisely the contribution to growth of each factor (ages, job
tenure and so on).   In addition, there are a number of other
features of the British economy - such as the switching on and off of
incomes policy - whose relevance may be examined without the use of
elaborate techniques.   Furthermore we have to consider some unquant-
ifiable but possibly important factors, such as the changing attitudes of workers and employers.

In order to see the issues in context, it is useful to begin by des-
cribing how government policies towards fringes have evolved over
the years, and to assess in the light of what evidence is available
how far they have been influential.   In the subsequent section we
consider the impact on fringes of various developments in the British
economy.   Finally we examine briefly the relevance and impact of
changing workers' preferences.

Government Policies

Since the Second World War, United Kingdom governments have been
committed, some more wholeheartedly than others, to the principles of
the welfare state.   Social and political attitudes towards fringe
benefits, however - many of which are close substitutes for state
welfare - do not necessarily reflect such a fundamental philosophical
stance.   Nonetheless, in a rather piecemeal way, government policies
have for a long time implicitly or explicitly favoured the expansion
of fringes.   Even Labour Governments during their three spells in
power have found few contradictions between their support for expanding social welfare and the rise of work-linked welfare schemes.

Governments have fostered various fringe benefits in both negative and positive ways. To begin with they have done very little so far to prevent the rising use of fringes as a device for promoting internal labour markets.

They have never interfered with companies' rights to give service-related holidays and sick pay. And until the 1970s nothing was done to combat the loss of pension rights by early leavers from occupational schemes, despite the fact that the problem had been discussed on and off since the 1930s, (Green, 1982a). Indeed, by disallowing the return of employers' contributions to quitting workers, governments have frequently reinforced firms' holds over their workforces. The Phillips Committee in 1955 failed to recommend legislation. The first steps towards a legal requirement for pensions to be preserved or transferable came with the Social Security Act 1973, followed by Labour's Social Security Pensions Act 1975. But this has imposed only a small degree of preservation, and it remains true that enormous penalties are imposed on those who quit early from their pension schemes. (Some proposed legislation for 1984 may partially reduce these penalties; we discuss this below in Chapter 8.)

Fringes have also been encouraged in positive ways, by the provision of a favourable tax environment and through incomes policies and other legislation.

(i) Tax Policies
Private pensions, in fact, have been encouraged for over sixty years. The fiscal framework was laid down first in two measures, the 1918 Income Tax Act and the 1921 Finance Act. These have now been consolidated with subsequent measures to allow tax exemptions up to certain limits on both the employer's and the employee's contributions. The income and capital gains from pension funds are also exempt, so the only tax paid is on the benefits paid out later to pensioners. Sick pay schemes have also been fiscally favoured, to some extent. Although tax is payable on sick pay, employers have been able to purchase insurance without paying tax on the premiums. Now, from 1983 onwards, they are not only favoured, they are compulsory. As for paid holidays, the income tax framework may have encouraged them, though we doubt whether this has been a conscious policy. Although pay while on leave is taxed in the normal way, the leisure time itself is not taxed. If the choice is between offering the worker one extra day's holiday and an increase of the equivalent of a day's wages, he or she may prefer the former since no extra taxes will be payable. Unlike in other European countries, there have however, been in general no legal requirements to provide a minimum period of leave.

Other fringes have also been favoured by special tax exemptions. There are some, such as canteens, luncheon vouchers, share purchase schemes, company sports facilities, day nurseries that have been exempt for a long time. Others, such as cheap loans, have been favoured in the past but not now while private medical insurance, for example, used not to be favoured but is now for the 'low-paid' worker. For those fringes that are not exempt, the tax-assessable benefits value is often much less than the real value of benefits received. For the 'low-paid' (remuneration less than £8,500 a year in 1982/3), only the second-hand cash value is taxed, which in many cases is zero. The high paid (above £8,500) are normally taxed according to the cost incurred by the employer.

But there is a major exception to this: company cars. Rather than assessing these also at cost, the Inland Revenue have adopted sets of rules which mean that the effective rates of taxation are extra-ordinarily low. Conservative estimates suggest that, for example, the 50% marginal tax rate payer will only effectively pay between 17 and 21% of the value of the car depending on its size.[1] Our own estimates (based on the AA scales of running costs) in Chapter 2 would put the effective tax rates lower. These figures also suggest that tax advantages have been increasing since the mid 1970s but it is difficult to be sure as it depends on estimates of the changing costs of cars of various sizes as well as changing marginal tax rates at different income levels. However, we have little hesitation in attributing the continuous growth of company cars over the last two decades primarily to the vast tax concessions afforded them.

How far can tax policy account for the growth of other fringe bene-fits? It is well known that tax rates have increased in Britain, as elsewhere, over a number of years. For example, the average direct tax rate rose from 11.3% in 1961 to 20% in 1976,[2] while the marginal tax rate for a male non-manual employee earning twice the average income of non manual males, went up from 49% in 1963 to 55% in 1976.

There is no doubt this must have been part of the reason for the growth of many fringes. Such an influence will be in accord with a widespread view, based both on economic reasoning and evidence from surveys of company practices, that the tax advantage of fringe bene-fits is an important influence on their spread, especially in the case of higher paid employees.[3]

However this was by no means the only cause and in some cases it may not have been particularly important. To begin with, the growth of fringes seems too large and widespread to be explicable by fiscal environment alone. If this were the overriding factor, the wage variable in our cross-section analyses would have been a more import-ant determinant of fringes.[4] As it is, it showed an impact in the case of some fringes but only a small one, and some of this could be due to other factors besides the implied tax advantage. Second, there are some fringes where it is obvious that tax has not been a relevant factor: for example private medical insurance grew most rapidly before it gained tax advantages, while day nurseries which are tax-exempt have not substantially grown. Third, our cross-section evidence also pointed to major features of the labour market, suggesting that changes in these also will have had an influence.

93

(ii) Incomes Policies

Incomes policies are primarily devices for reducing wage inflation,
but they have also been used to try to influence certain types of
fringe benefit. By allowing certain fringes to be negotiated out-
side the limitations of the pay restraint rules, governments aimed
to encourage private welfare. Thus the 1973 Pay Code permitted
pension increases and holiday increases up to the limit of three
weeks, presumably because the government of the time wished to emphasise these types of welfare. Later, the various incomes policies
of the 1974-9 Labour government excluded improvements in sick pay as
well as pensions from the pay guidelines, but included holiday rises.

It makes economic sense that, in so far as an incomes policy is a
real constraint on wage and salary bargaining, employers and
employees will use such fringes to get round the restrictions. It
is sometimes suggested that the 1970s policies brought about a major
change in benefit strategies, but this seems to be going rather far
given that most fringes were supposed to be included within the pay
rules. But since the value of many fringes is often ill-defined
and undisclosed - for example, it was easy to redefine the 'essential
usage' of company cars[5] - it is possible that many fringes could have
received a boost. Such loopholes are more probable for high paid
employees in the upper strata of the primary labour markets, who were
likely to contemplate moving jobs in order to improve their salaries.
To them the flat-rate elements in the successive stages of incomes
policy were particularly unwelcome in that they meant an erosion in
income differentials. In their case it was also easier for an
employer to introduce selective and rather unconventional fringe
benefits. There were questions in parliament asking whether the incomes policies were not being widely flouted through the use of company expense accounts and other devices. In the mid 1970s, the
government had proposed economic but no legal sanctions against companies which broke the pay codes, and detection of these deals would
have been almost impossible for high paid employees with individually
negotiated remuneration.

However, beyond the anecdotal and casual level, it is not easy to
substantiate these propositions by looking at the growth path of
fringes. Figure 1 charts the limited annual time series that exist
for a few fringes. It can be seen that the percentage of executives
with subsidised meals and with free medical insurance did receive
jolts in 1966-67 and in 1972-3, coinciding with severe incomes
policies. But other incomes policies are not shown to have any obvious effect. Meanwhile the rise of pension contributions - which
were, after all, the main legal loophole in the 1970s policies - was
not apparently affected at all. Some further evidence is provided
in Figures 2 and 3. It is for example clear that the tremendous
growth in private medical insurance cannot be attributed to incomes
policies and the rest of the evidence is rather inconclusive.

If the pay policies had had a very substantial effect it would have
been more obvious in the diagrams. Instead, fringe benefits were

94

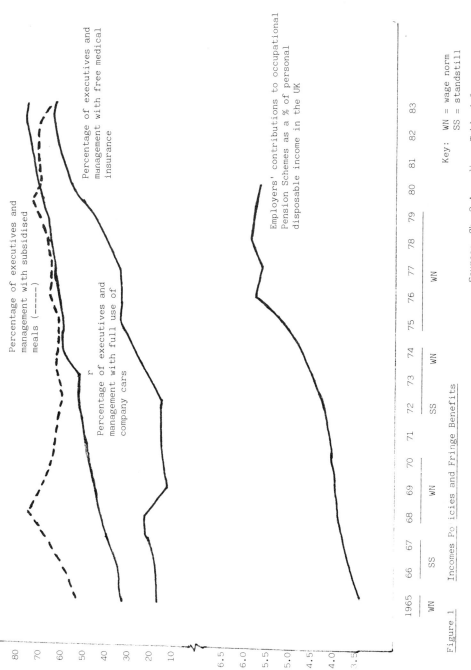

Percentage of executives and management with subsidised meals (-----)

Percentage of executives and management with free medical insurance

Percentage of executives and management with full use of company cars

Employers' contributions to occupational Pension Schemes as a % of personal disposable income in the UK

Key: WN = wage norm
      SS = standstill

Source: Ch. 2 Appendix, Table A.9

Figure 1   Incomes Policies and Fringe Benefits

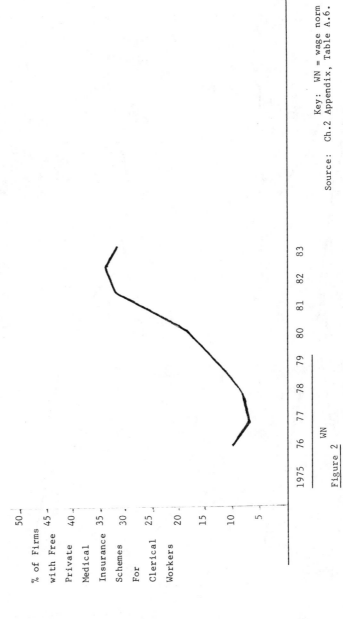

% of Firms
with Free

Private
Medical

Insurance

Schemes

For

Clerical

Workers

50 —
45 —
40 —
35 —
30 —
25 —
20 —
15 —
10 —
5 —

1975 76 77 78 79 80 81 82 83

WN

Figure 2

Incomes Policies and Fringe Benefits

Source: Key: WN = wage norm
         Ch.2 Appendix, Table A.6.

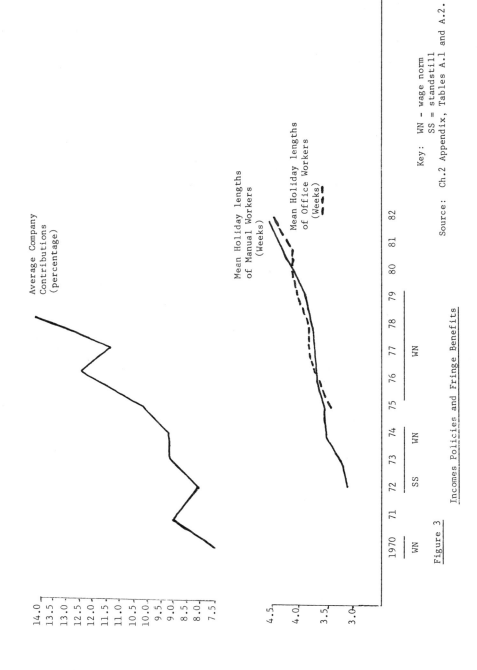

Pension Benefit Contributions in Managerial Jobs

Average Company
Contributions
(percentage)

14.0
13.5
13.0
12.5
12.0
11.5
11.0
10.5
10.0
9.5
9.0
8.5
8.0
7.5

Mean Holiday lengths
of Manual Workers
(Weeks)

Mean Holiday lengths
of Office Workers
(Weeks)

4.5
4.0
3.5
3.0

1970 71 72 73 74 75 76 77 78 79 80 81 82

WN   SS   WN   WN

Figure 3   Incomes Policies and Fringe Benefits

Key: WN - wage norm
      SS = standstill

Source: Ch.2 Appendix, Tables A.1 and A.2.

rising anyway. However, it remains likely that they must have altered the balance of remuneration to some extent, in the ill-defined ways mentioned above which would not necessarily show up in the statistics. It is also possible that the policies may have served to change trade unions' attitudes to bargaining over some fringes - if so the effect would have been to raise them not during the policy period but some time later.

(iii) Other Policies

Other pieces of employment legislation had some impact on fringes. For example, the payments of fringes are, like wages, subject to the Sex Discrimination Act 1975 and the Race Relations Act 1976, while occupational pensions were constrained to provide a minimal level of preserved pensions under the Social Security Pensions Act 1975. In addition, by making some benefits universal and compulsory, legislation effectively stops them being 'fringe' benefits in the normal sense. An example is maternity leave. Prior to the 1975 Employment Protection Act, a relatively small percentage of companies provided maternity rights. Today the large majority of firms simply conform to the requirements of the Act without granting anything over that statutory minimum.[6] Nevertheless, the impact of the law is severely restrained by the lack of any improvement in childcare facilities and nurseries. In Britain public provision for this need is still highly underdeveloped and inferior in comparison with the rest of Europe. Thus it seems likely that this and other legislation have not substantially altered the growth of fringes.

However governments can affect fringes in other ways, through their influence on related parts of the economy. A prime example is the rapid growth of private medical insurance, to the level of 4.2 million insured people in 1982 (see Chapter 2). Most of the growth has been through group company subscriptions. Apart from the reduced cost of group schemes and more aggressive marketing, the reasons normally given for this growth are the deteriorating service and longer waiting lists of the National Health Service compared to the rapid medical treatment at times convenient for companies available in the private sector. Since 1979 the Conservative Government has adopted a sympathetic and encouraging attitude towards private medicine, for example easing the construction of private hospitals by lifting the NHS veto, and allowing NHS consultants to earn up to 10% of their income from private practice, and so on. In the face of opposition from the trade union movement, the government's influence on this benefit is shown by the sharp jump in its growth from 1979 onwards, illustrated in Figure 1.

Economic and Other Factors

The analysis so far has suggested that while government strategy has had some effect, by no means all the growth of fringes can be explained in this way. In the past decades the British economy has of course developed in a number of ways, and so we now turn to see how far the growth can be understood in terms of the major economic factors which we have emphasised in previous chapters.

(i) Wages

Between the first government survey of labour costs in 1964 and the
latest one in 1981 most people became more prosperous.   For example,
in manufacturing industries real annual wages rose by about 35%.
Our evidence has suggested a small effect of wages on pensions, sick
pay, holidays and some of the lesser fringes.   Probably this partly
reflects tax and other factors.   But it is reasonable also to
attribute the rise of fringes over the years at least partly to
their having an income elasticity above one.   As standards of
living rise employees on the whole prefer or are more willing to
accept a changing pattern of remuneration that automatically provides
for relatively more leisure time, better coverage for old-age, sickness, maternity needs, improved medical care, and recreational and
cultural facilities.

(ii) Tenure and Unemployment

Between 1968 and 1981 the turnover rate per 4 weeks period in manufacturing industries fell from about 3% to 1.4%.[7]   This tells us
that it is very likely that the proportions of long-tenured workers
rose in most industries.   Our evidence revealed a strong association between tenure and fringes, born of a two-way relationship.
Long tenure leads to high fringe benefits, given the way that many
schemes are designed; but in addition high fringes can serve to
reduce mobility.   The association is particularly strong for pensions and sick pay and it is notable that voluntary social welfare
payments are the fringe category whose costs have increased the most
over the years.

Meanwhile, from the mid 1960s to 1983 the official unemployment rate
rose from below 2% to about 13%.   This rise is associated with the
increase in tenure, and the effect is reinforcing on fringes.   It
tends to be disproportionately the low-tenured workers in secondary
labour markets who lose their jobs.   If the incidence of unemployment is higher among manual part-time, female and low-tenure employees (including school-leavers who would under different economic
circumstances have been employed) the effect is a rise in the
average fringe benefit component of remuneration.[8]

A further influence on the level of fringes in aggregate derives from
the changing industrial structure.   Some of the most rapidly expanding industries in the post-war period, such as insurance, banking and
finance, and professional and scientific services, as well as the
public sector are characterised by a long-tenured labour force.   On
the other hand declining industries such as Textiles and Clothing and
Footwear exhibit on average a substantially shorter tenure of employment.   (See Appendix, Table A1.)

Taking these factors together, there is clearly a strong association
between the rise of tenure-related fringes and the changing tenure
structure of British industry.

(iii) <u>Size</u>
Although our evidence revealed a strong association of many fringes
with size of establishment, this does not on the whole help to
account for the growth of fringes.   In most manufacturing industries
the average size fell a little while the proportion in establishments
of less than 100 workers rose from 18.4% in 1968 to 24.4% in 1978.

On the other hand, the structure of industry changed in significant
ways.   Gas, Electricity and Water, had much the largest average
size (1,578 employees per establishment in 1978) and it expanded
much faster than other industries;   meanwhile Construction, for
example, has relatively small sized units and rose much less than
average.   A further consideration is that with increased market
concentration of industries average firm size has risen despite the
fall in establishment size.   However we have no separate evidence
on the effect of firm size on fringes.

On balance we do not consider this to have been a significant factor
behind the growth of fringes.

(iv)   <u>Type of Worker</u>
In most industries there has been a decline in the proportions of
lower status workers.   For example, between 1964 and 1981 the percentage of non-manuals in manufacturing industries rose from 26% to
31% and from 34% to 50% in Gas, Electricity and Water.   (See Appendix
Table A2.).   Moreover there has been a shift to public sector employment and to financial and service sectors, all of which have
relatively high numbers of non-manual workers.   Our cross-section
analysis implied that social class was in most cases a strong independent cause of high fringes.   So the rise of non-manual workers,
although not enormous, must explain a fair deal of the growth of
fringes that has occurred.

By contrast, none of it can be reasonably attributed to changes in
the ratios of male and female workers.   These stayed broadly constant in manufacturing industries while in service sectors the proportions of females rose.   From our cross-section evidence, this
would imply no effect on sick pay and if anything a small fall in
pensions.   Similarly, the proportions of part-time workers have
everywhere expanded slightly, but even though our results were somewhat conflicting, this could not plausibly account for any of the
growth of fringes.

(v)   <u>Union Membership</u>
While we find a small association of unionisation with a few fringes,
we considered it unlikely that this was the result of conscious bargaining in the past, except in the case of holidays.   Only a few of
the non-manufacturing unions seriously bargained over pensions in the
1960s.   So while there was a rise in the proportions in unions (44%
in 1968 to 53% in 1977, subsequently falling) it is unlikely that
much of the fringe benefit growth was due to the growth of union
membership.

More recently, in view of the increasing importance of fringes in the remuneration package, trade unions could no longer afford to ignore them. At the same time, there was increasing regulation of employment matters in the 1970s. Determining remuneration became a more complex process, and unions found they could perform a useful role for existing and potential members in providing information and in bargaining for complicated benefit schemes. A number of hand-books for union officials were published as, with the change in economic and political climate, unions were obliged to drop their traditional antipathy towards fringe benefits.[9] However, they have, not surprisingly, remained hostile to certain fringes, notably company cars with their glaring inequities and private medical insurance with its undermining of the NHS.

Given this recent increased involvement it would be surprising if unions have not had some effect recently on the levels of fringe benefits. It is likely for example that, by aggressive bargaining and by their emphasis on cutting work time, they have been responsible for some of the increased holidays of manual workers which has to some extent enabled them to catch up non-manuals. However there is no independent evidence on this hypothesis.

(vi) Other Factors

Finally it may be recalled that, independent of the economic factors so far mentioned, some industries tended to have relatively high and some low fringes. This was due to the particular character of those industries. With the exception of Mining and Quarrying, the 'high' industries are ones which have expanded the fastest, (especially since they tend to be in the public sector where much of the expanded employment has been located). 'Low' industries, such as Clothing and Footwear, Textiles, and Timber and Furniture have all grown by less than the average for all manufacturing. Such structural changes must therefore account for a portion of the growth of fringes in the aggregate.

Summary and Concluding Remarks

Our analysis has highlighted several economic developments which must have helped to raise the levels of fringe benefits relative to wages. The most important of these were the rising levels of job tenure in industries and associated with this the rise in unemployment, the rise in the proportions of non-manuals in the workforce, the general increase in incomes and standards of living and the changing structures of British industry.[10]

Together with successive governments' practices of providing a favourable tax environment, with incomes policies and other policies in related fields which we considered in the first section, we have a reasonable picture of why fringes have grown so much.

Changing Preferences?

Yet some commentators refer often to yet another cause: the changing attitudes of employees. Thus for example it was concluded from a

British Institute of Management survey of employees views that "certain benefits, such as pensions, had become 'institutionalised' - that is they are regarded as a basic entitlement or condition of employment to which all were entitled rather than as 'fringe' benefits - to the point where they are taken for granted when offered but, when not offered, create a feeling of deprivation".[11] In a similar vein, the 1982 Alfred Marks Survey of fringe benefits for office staff stated (p.51): "It is evident that to the majority of employees, fringe benefits are a very necessary and important part of the compensation package available to them. They may show little overt appreciation for the majority of benefits, but just try to take them away!" Implicitly it is argued that the growth of fringes is partly a reflection of workers' attitudes towards them becoming more favourable.

But while it is plausible that preferences for fringes have indeed changed over the years, the problem with this approach lies in identifying whether this is a separate and independent cause or, instead, merely an effect of growing fringes. After all it is hardly surprising if an employee's attitude changes in response to receiving, say, a company car. He or she becomes accustomed to the status symbol it represents and learns the value of the tax exemption.

There is no evidence that permits us to identify any cases where the preference change came first.

Nonetheless, the relevance of changing attitudes should not be ignored, and indeed the idea is akin to the 'Relative Income' Theory[12] in the study of consumer behaviour. This theory proposes that consumers' wants are changed by contact with other peoples' consumption behaviour - either through a 'demonstration' effect or through a desire to emulate them. Alternatively consumers may be influenced by their own past consumption habits. These same hypotheses may be applied to the demand for fringes. Thus, for example, it may be proposed that employees form a desire to belong to an occupational pension scheme as a result of observing other workers with this benefit. Moreover a ratchet effect is implied whereby, once achieved, workers would feel more of a loss if they were deprived of a fringe benefit than if they had never had it in the first place. A further possibility is that attitude changes interact with the other factors and with policy changes. For example, the passing of employment legislation or of incomes policies may draw workers' attention to the existence and value of certain fringes, as well as pushing unions to start bargaining over them.

An important empirical implication of such hypotheses is that there would be a lagged response to policy changes or to movements of any of the independent variables.[13] To look for this one would need an adequate set of time series data on both fringes and other variables, something which does not exist at present. Given that, the hypotheses remain interesting but unproven.

Future Growth

A final point of interest surrounds the question as to whether fringe benefits will continue to grow or whether they are likely to come up against limits. We would expect the same economic factors that have been important till now to be relevant also in the future. But what happens will depend on changes both in the various factors and in government policies. For the moment it is simplest to assume no change in policy. If we also make the plausible assumptions that the proportions of non-manual workers will continue to grow, that job-tenure will rise (given a low voluntary turnover in the face of high unemployment), that the size of firms and establishments does not substantially fall and that real wages either rise or stay constant, it is likely that fringe benefits will continue to grow in importance.

Of course there is probably an ultimate limit to the expansion of some fringes, in that the demand for them may reach a saturation point. In that case, if growth were to continue for those who have not reached that point while it is suspended for those on already high levels, there would be a gradual catching-up process and reduction in the inequality of fringes. It is possible that a process of this sort underlies the narrowing of the gap between manual and non-manual workers' holidays (see Chapter 2). However there is little or no evidence of any equalisation of other fringes and indeed the conclusion of Chapter 2 was that it is likely that the overall inequality of fringes has been increasing. The ranking of industries in 1981, according to their average shares of voluntary social welfare payments, benefits in kind and subsidised services, is not much different from what it was in 1964 (see Appendix, Table A1) and there are no signs of industries reaching saturation point yet. For top managers and executives, there is some levelling off in the proportions receiving company cars and some other fringes (Chapter 2, Table A9), but there is always room for improving further the value of these benefits for example by raising the size of the car or the firm's contributions to their running costs.

In short we do not expect that fringe benefit shares will stop growing, let alone start falling, in the absence of any policy changes. However, it is clear that government policies do have a substantial effect on fringes. In the next and final chapter we examine the grounds for recommending new policies.

Footnotes

1. Potter (1983).

2. See Economic Trends, Jan. 1977 and Jan. 1980.

3. See, for example, Murlis (1978).

4. This statement is conditional on the assumption that the tax advantage is equally relevant in explaining both the distribution and the growth of fringe benefits.

5. Murlis (1976b), p.10.

6. Cunningham (1981), pp.133-4.

7. Average of discharge of engagement rates. See Employment Gazette, February 1984.

8. If on the other hand job losses are more prevalent among those near retirement age the opposite effect should be expected, in view of the higher fringe benefit component for this age group.

9. For example: Cunningham (1981); Ward (1981).

10. An attempt was made to confirm these conclusions using formal statistical techniques by pooling the industry data from the six labour cost surveys running from 1964 to 1981. The hypotheses were tested using a linear model that assumed a constant structural relationship in order to be able to combine cross-section and time-series observations. However, despite considerable effort, the results obtained were not very useful. Although the wages coefficient was generally positive, the parameter estimates of other variables were unstable - they varied a lot depending on the specifications used and the variables included. This was essentially due to the deficiencies of the data. In particular, the dependent variable was aggregated at the level of Industry Order, there being no available breakdowns by size or by MLH. Also, many independent variables were poorly specified.

11. Murlis (1978), p.4.

12. Duesenberry (1948).

13. Moreover, as suggested earlier, this might account for the failure to identify any immediate effect on incomes policies.

Appendix: SOME DATA ON FRINGES AND CHANGING INDUSTRIAL AND EMPLOYMENT STRUCTURE

Table A.1. Fringes by Industry 1964-1981, and Tenure

	(1) Fringes+ as ratio of labour costs, 1964, %	(2) Rank of column (1)	(3) Fringes+ as ratio of labour costs, 1981, %	(4) Rank of column (3)	(5) Employment Change, * 1964 to 1981 (%)	(6) Tenure **
Mining and Quarrying	10.3	1	16.6	1	-48.8	85
Chemical and Allied Industries	8.3	2	11.1	3	-22.6	80
Gas, Electricity and Water	7.3	3	14.6	2	-17.9	85
Food, Drink and Tobacco	6.3	4	8.2	4	-23.8	67
Paper, Printing and Publishing	3.9	5	6.3	9	-21.7	74
Metal Manufacture	3.6	6	7.8	5	-47.6	75
Vehicles	3.5	7	7.7	6	-28.2	81
Other Manufacturing	3.3	8	6.4	7	-19.6	65
Metal goods not elsewhere specified	3.2	9	5.7	11	-	68
Bricks, pottery, glass, cement &c.	3.2	9	6.4	7	-39.6	66
Textiles	3.1	11	4.1	14	-56.1	62
Shipbuilding & Marine Eng.	2.4	12	6.0	10	-32.8	66
Construction	2.3	13	4.3	12	-31.6	43

105

	(1) Fringes+ as ratio of labour costs, 1964, %	(2) Rank of column (1)	(3) Fringes+ as ratio of labour costs 1981, %	(4) Rank of column (3)	(5) Employment Change, * 1964 to 1981 (%)	(6) Tenure **
Leather, Leathergoods and Fur	2.2	14	3.7	15	-50.2	-
Clothing and Footwear	2.1	15	2.9	16	-44.5	68

+ Voluntary Social Welfare Payments, Benefits in Kind and Subsidised Services.
* measured from June 1964 to June 1981; (Source: Employment Gazette December 1968 and November 1982).
** percentage of jobs held in 1968, that did not end before 1978; (Source: Main, 1982).

Table A.2.   Labour Force Composition

	Proportion of Non-manual workers in labour force		Proportion of females in labour force		Proportion of part-time workers in labour force	
	1964	1981	1964	1981	1968	1981
All Manufacturing Industries	26	31	30	29	5	6.5
Mining and Quarrying	16	15	3	6	1	1.2
Construction	18	28	5	8	1	3.4
Gas, Electricity and Water	34	50	12	20	2	4.3
Insurance and Banking	95	-	43	54	7	7.2

Source: Employment Gazette;   various issues

CHAPTER 8

FRINGE BENEFIT POLICY

Introduction

Even though successive governments' policies have made a substantial difference to the growth and distribution of fringes, their approaches have tended to be piecemeal. For example, some fringes are taxed while others for no good reason are not. The only consistent rationale for some of these exemptions is that the collection cost in the case of low-valued fringes may be too high in relation to revenue. Thus it may make sense to allow exemptions for the low paid if this reduces sufficiently the number of assessors that the Inland Revenue has to employ. Apart from that, the various concessions seem to have arisen haphazardly without any overall rationale. Specific reasons can be found for some individual fringes, as are exemplified by the exceptions which were purposely declared at various stages during the 1970's incomes policies. But even these were never openly justified.

There is a continual tension between the promotion of social and private welfare benefits both between and within the two main political parties. Moreover, their actual policies are frequently not consistent with their stated intentions. Both Labour and Conservative governments made pronouncements against non-wage benefits and their expansion in the 1970s but they were not followed up by any serious attempts to abolish or even substantially reduce their tax advantages.[1]

Piecemeal policies may have had their specific advantages in promoting government aims in various areas, but the consequence of not having a consistent overall approach is that a number of problems have arisen, which have harmed the economy directly or have tended to frustrate the aims of social and economic policies. In view of the current importance of fringes in the nation's labour cost bill, and of the problems to which the policies so far have given rise, it would be desirable now to consider and to formulate a general fringe benefit policy for the future. In what follows in this chapter we offer a suggested approach based on our own investigations. After discussing the context of such a policy we state the principles upon which it should be based - equality, openness and efficiency - and consider how, in the light of our analytical and empirical results, fiscal and other policies should be framed. We conclude by evaluating the impact of the most recent change in policy: the introduction of Statutory Sick Pay in April 1983.

The Policy Context

Any new policy must take into account the effects of fringes on the economy and their interrelationship with other economic and social policies.

(i) To begin with, fringes affect labour markets: as we have argued they are often the instruments with which employers attempt to segment and divide the labour force, creating barriers to mobility. Our empirical results are consistent with this view, for we have shown how fringes tend to be high on the whole where wages are relatively high, in large firms, for long-tenured and full-time workers where turnover is correspondingly low - in short, where internal labour markets are present. Thus fringes help to create a divided workforce and to perpetuate inequalities.

This is not to suggest, of course, that inequalities could be removed by abolishing fringes! Without them, it would still be possible for employers to restrict mobility in other ways, such as high wages or improved working conditions for long-serving employees; but their ability to do so would, to some extent, be impaired.

(ii) Secondly, fringes can have a crucial impact on other aspects of the economy if they become substantial enough. This has already happened with pensions and company cars and it could happen with other fringes as well. Pension funds have come to wield considerable power in financial markets, throught their sheer size. As Minns (1980) demonstrates, most funds have come to be controlled by banks, and their investment has been disproportionately concentrated on large firms and on the financial companies. Whether one feels such influence is good or bad, the fact that they do have a structural impact on the economy is clear. A further possible effect is on the level of other types of saving which are stimulated or substituted by the growth of pensions: whatever happens affects the aggregate level of savings in the economy.[2] As for company cars, any substantial subsidy is certain to have major effects on the transport industry as a whole. In Britain, mainly for reasons of appearance rather than objective cost advantages, companies have in the past tended to favour British made cars and new ones at that. Recently the presumption in favour of British has become less important (see below), but it remains true that if cars are to be provided through companies there will be a tendency to meet the demands of the company car purchaser rather than the individual. In the past this had led to demands for larger cars than individuals appear to prefer for themselves - partly reflecting a greater element of conspicuous consumption by companies. The average engine size of (registered) company cars is 1.61 litres compared to 1.38 litres for private cars. In shifting the balance towards larger engine sizes, company cars have conditioned the development of the domestic motor industry, as well as raising the rate of petrol consumption, possibly by as much as 10%.[3]

(iii) Thirdly, the development of fringes has direct implications
for the success of other government policies, both social and
economic.

The existence of private pensions has been partly stimulated by the
failure of state pensions to expand fast enough, particularly for
all but the low-paid.   But also the causation runs the other way.
Pressure to expand state pensions for so long in the 1950s and 1969s
was absent partly because those groups in society, which have greater
political influence, (broadly encompassing higher paid workers and
managers and top civil servants) were able to rely on the growing
private pension sector to satisfy their own needs.   In future, any
policy for private pensions must imply a parallel one for state pensions.   As another example, any subsidy to company cars, as now
exists, must have repercussions on other transport policies: subsidies to roads affects the numbers of people that use the railways
and hence the size of the subsidy required there.

An increasing area of concern is the relationship between policy towards the National Health Service and the expansion of private medicine.   Although there was until 1982 no tax exemption when this was
provided as a fringe benefit the fact is that most of the expanded
demand for private beds and hospitals since 1979 has come from com-
pany-provided medical insurance schemes.   Policy towards this fringe
benefit must therefore reflect policy towards the NHS.   There are
two schools of thought here.   One, which is the basis of current
government policy, is that private medicine is additional to the NHS,
that it is more efficient, and that if anything it removes pressure
on its resources.   The other - to which we subscribe - is that it
takes away resources from the NHS and allows those with more wealth
to obtain better and earlier treatment at the expense of those who
cannot.   The main mechanism for this is that doctors and other medical workers, trained at the expense of the government, are induced
by higher wages and salaries to move into the private sector;   in
addition, private medicine is able to take advantage of the theoretical advances obtained from research in the public sector.   A further
important factor is that the political backing for improvements in
the deficient NHS is less likely to be forthcoming when the alternative of the private sector is flourishing.

Fringes have also posed problems for the enforcement of incomes
policies, and could do so still if they again become fashionable.
The precise amount of certain fringes received, such as pensions,
expense accounts, use of company car, and so on, are fairly easy to
conceal, if not from the tax collector at least from the rest of the
workforce.   Such tax evasion and avoidance raises the costs of pol-
icing, and leads to widespread suspicion that certain groups (usually
the high-paid) are getting away with it.

A further consideration, given the current fiscal situations that
governments find themselves in, is the tax revenue lost.   It is impossible to estimate this accurately because it depends on the assump-

tions made, particularly as to how individuals would react if the tax
exemptions were removed.   The Inland Revenue estimate of £5 billion
lost in 1983[4] from pension tax exemptions and Potter's (1983) estimated range of £700 million to £2.2 billion direct cost of company car
tax avoidance in 1983/4, compares with total income tax revenue of
under £31 billion in 1982/3.   However rough the calculations, the
sums involved are large.   Such 'tax-expenditures' apart from their
distributional impact, are not subject to the same controls and
evaluations as other forms of public expenditure; moreover they disadvantage the fiscal structure by narrowing the tax-base; (Pond,
1980).

Finally, as we have shown at several stages, fringes have also been
the proximate cause of greater inequality of remuneration.   Whether
this is counted as a 'problem' depends on the policy stance towards
equality which a particular government takes.   Kincaid (1973) shows
how the 1964 to 1970 Labour Governments delayed plans to reform the
pension system, and when the proposals eventually appeared as the
Crossman Plan in 1969 they revealed a much reduced commitment to
equality compared to the strategy prepared in the 1950's when out of
office.   In the event, the proposals were lost with the dissolution
of Parliament in 1970.   If any future government is to adopt an egalitarian stance towards incomes it will need to confront the problem
of fringes too.

Three Principles

Our policy proposals are premised on three underlying objectives:
euality, openness and efficiency.

The strategy for greater equality animates the idea of the 'welfare
state' and we take this as read.[5]   Company welfare policy should be
consistent with the same aim.   Second, openness is an important
principle, for without it social policies are likely in the long run
to lose public support.   In the case of company welfare policy, we
believe that what is or is not paid to employees should be openly
observable: only then can differences between peoples' remunerations
be rationally assessed.

Third, policies should aim for efficiency, particularly when this does
not conflict with equality or openness.   It is sometimes argued that
state intervention in the economy leads to inefficiency: that, for
example, social welfare payments reduce incentives and state industries
are poor because they are not constrained by the profit motive.   These
are false generalisations which we do not propose to deal with here.
But it is worth noting that policies which encourage private welfare
strategies can also create distortions in the market.   Employees are
discouraged from moving jobs, and they are provided with cheap benefits
which in the absence of tax reliefs they might not otherwise want.
Such distortions are arbitrary and inefficient, and should be removed
unless linked to a clear social policy objective.

Taking the 'Fringe' Out of Some 'Fringe Benefits'
Not all fringe benefits should be treated in the same way. It is
widely agreed that people have certain 'rights' at work - either
because they are a necessary aspect of being an employee, or because
they conform to certain humanitarian objectives or principles of
public responsibility. Many rights are embodied already in labour
laws: the right to redundancy pay, to be paid the same rate for the
same job regardless of race and sex, and so on. Some fringes come
into this category: they should be regarded as rights, and should
not be treated as 'fringe' benefits at all.

To begin with, all full-time workers should have the entitlement to
at least four weeks paid holiday annually. Some would disagree with
the number, but we believe most would assent that some holidays are
necessary. The benefit should be equally available to all as far as
possible, though it remains true that since the pace of work varies
for different groups of workers, some would need more holidays than
others. In Britain, without the help of laws substantial gains have
been achieved. Yet legislation to defend these gains would be helpful, as would legislation to ensure appropriate holiday rights for
part-time workers.

Paid sick leave should also be a guaranteed right, as it now is, on
basic humanitarian principles. An additional reason is that
employees who are ill with infectious diseases should be discouraged
from returning to work where their infection can spread. Sick pay
thus has external benefits to employers, other workers and to members
of the public, in addition to meeting the needs of the ill person.
While providing for sick workers has always been an ingredient of the
welfare state, responsibility for payment for the first eight weeks of
illnesses was changed in April 1983. Sickness benefits from the
state ceased, and employers were required to pay Statutory Sick Pay to
all employees, regardless of whether they previously had an occupational sick pay scheme. We review below the effects of this change.

Similarly, short term leave for bereavement or for family sickness
should be a guaranteed right, as should paternity and maternity leave.
The last of these has legal backing at present, and so have certain
other forms of leave entitlement (for jury and public service) though
there is no entitlement to pay. We would also support a move to make
sabbatical leave equally available for all. This should be quite
possible in the age of modern high technology, though we judge it
unlikely to find acceptance unless trade unions take up the demand.

If a worker has to move house as a requirement of a job, considerable
expense is incurred. If not recompense is made, he or she might be
forced to quit, thereby losing redundancy payments. Hence, we
believe all workers have a right to financial compensation for necessary moves - otherwise some companies could get rid of workers without
assuming their financial responsibilities towards them.

Finally, we propose that all employers above a minimum size should be required to provide creches for the care of young children. This is particularly important if the social objective of equality for women in society, and particularly in the labour market, is to be achieved. Lack of creche and nursery facilities prohibits many women from being in the labour market after bearing children, in this society where women are still charged with most of the child-rearing burden. At the moment creches remain a fringe benefit available only to the few. Yet they have the advantage over state or private non-work-based facilities that they enable parents to be at paid work yet not separated for long periods from their children; moreover in many cases it saves making two separate journeys in the morning, one to leave a child and the other to work. Few measures would do more to create greater social equality than this simple one we propose, yet it is questionable whether public attitudes are ready to contemplate the right to work-based child care, given that it is currently so uncommon. Trade unions should be encouraged to respond to this need by giving it priority in their bargaining.

To sum up this section, we have delineated certain types of benefits which we argue should no longer be regarded as 'fringe' but as rights at work. In doing so we are drawing attention to their social (as opposed to purely private) advantages. They are benefits which should be available for all workers and are by their nature best provided by the employer. Legislation should be used to ensure the attainment of these rights, though in some cases it is likely that they may be gained more quickly through the collective bargaining process.

Policy on Other Fringe Benefits
There is no justification for encouraging the provision of other fringe benefits, through favourable tax exemptions and other policies, where there is no particular social gain or where there is no need for them to be provided at work.[6]

(a)   Taxation:
Our empirical results have shown that, apart from the influence of other variables, income is usually a significant determinant of the proportion that fringes bear in total remuneration. This is consistent with the widely held presumption that fringes are stimulated by tax examptions since those on higher incomes pay higher marginal tax rates. Removal of tax privileges would lead to a rise in the fraction of remuneration paid as wages. At the same time it would lead to a reduction in inequality, since current tax avoidance is disproportionately available to the rich.

This would not, in all probability, lead to the disappearance of fringe benefits altogether, either immediately or in the long run; nor would it be intended to. There are a number of fringes which it may still be advantageous for firms to provide, due to economies of scale. Our empirical work has consistently shown the importance of size with several benefits. Partly this reflects the presence of internal

112

labour markets in large companies but it also reflects increasing returns to scale. For example, the provision of canteens may cost too much for small firms, but for large ones it could be more efficient to provide meals at the workplace than for workers to have to go to local cafes. Although their prevalence would probably be reduced by removal of tax exemptions canteens for workers and expensive meals for directors would still exist. If employees are prepared to pay the price at which firms find it worthwhile to provide them, they will still flourish. In other words, let the market work, for there is no good reason to interfere with it here. A similar argument applies to such things as the provision of discounts on company goods and services.

Abolishing tax privileges would also provide social gains from improved efficiency. It is impossible to say exactly how much, but some idea of the possible gains from ending company pensions schemes and administering all pensions through the state can be gleaned from the fact that in 1979 there were roughly 90,000 separate schemes provided by 85,000 employers. Of these, 60,000 had less than 10 members and on average less than 4. The unit administrative costs were therefore relatively high. As an indication, public sector schemes' expenses were under 0.7% of their total expenses in 1975, whereas in the private sector the figure was nearly 7%, ten times as much.[7]

Those who are less concerned about the gross inequalities of the current ptovision of occupational pensions may argue that their extra administration cost is worth bearing, point to the advantages of the financial discipline of the capital markets yet to the financial security provided by the funded scheme. But expanding the state pensions sector is the only real option for ensuring adequate pensions for all the aged, and this need not be done at the expense of the extra savings of those who can afford it. The philosophy of collective provision is that needs are paramount: that the retired person's pension should not depend on the prosperity in thecapitalmarket of any one fund. The government's 'pay-as-you-go' system naturally depends on the future solvency of the state and its ability to raise taxes, which in turn depends on the economy remaining viable. In this sense, neither state nor private pensions are 100% secure, for both types rest on economic prosperity.

Efficiency gains would also come from reducing tax privileges for other fringes, notably company cars. It is both equitable and efficient to subsidise British Rail and other public transport systems, on the grounds of providing a service and of gaining the externalities from less congested roads. But there are no social or economic reasons why company cars and hence private road transport should receive a heavy subsidy, greater as it is now according to some estimates than that paid to British Rail. Its removal would go some way towards making the private cost of car travel approximate more closely the true social cost.

Apart from these equality and efficiency gains from removing tax exemptions, an automatic by-product would be a considerable rise in tax revenues, and removal of one of the many anomalous 'tax-expenditures' which are never subjected to adequate public scrutiny.

(b)   Harmonisation:
Removal of tax privileges would go a long way but would not be enough to achieve all social objectives. Our empirical work has shown that there remains a considerable advantage, as far as fringes are concerned, in being a non-manual worker, and even more in being of higher status. This increases the proportion of remuneration paid as fringes independent of the simultaneous impact of higher incomes which usually go along with the status. The advantage does not derive from tax avoidance and so it would remain unless further action is taken.

These differences between manual and non-manual workers are often concealed - for example, pension scheme differences remain widespread yet they are not obvious to those at work who do not know how pensioners fare after retirement. In accordance with our principle of openness, as well as with the objective of greater equality, we therefore advocate measures to harmonise the treatment of all types of workers. Such harmonisation can be, and has been, vigorously pursued by collective bargaining. This has been the case with paid holidays. However, in other cases we believe it will be necessary to insist legally that fringes are equally available to all employees regardless of status.

(c)   Mobility Policy: Preserving Pension Rights:
Where they remain fringes, being less open and observable than wages, could still be used as a device for establishing internal labour markets, that is for restricting labour mobility. A case in point is the problem of the early leaver in pension schemes. Although the removal of tax privileges would lessen the value of occupational pension schemes they would remain for some time. The penalty costs imposed on early leavers are enormous. They either prevent mobility when it otherwise would occur, which is inefficient; or if a worker quits anyway it leads to gross unfairness. Due to lack of information, this problem would remain even if there were no tax avoidance.

Since there has been much public debate on these issues it is appropriate to comment briefly on them here. The present government has a programme for tackling the 'early leaver' problem, but their proposals only go some of the way, and maybe not very far, towards solving it. The Occupational Pensions Board (OPB) reported in 1981, and recommended legislation to ensure some degree of protection beyond the Guaranteed Minimum Pension (GMP). Their proposal was that the pension benefit above the GMP of the early leaver be compulsorily raised by the rate of earnings inflation or 5% per annum, whichever is the less. The government delayed for two years in the hope of voluntary action by the pensions industry. The response (as usual) not forthcoming, legislation was proposed in a consultative document and will probably be brought before Parliament in late 1984 - with the one main change that price inflation rather than earnings inflation is to be used as the criterion.

In addition, it is possible that before too long, individuals will be given a right to transfer the value of their pension rights to a new scheme; though this will not affect further the costs to the individual of quitting, since the value of the transfer is to be equal to the actuarially calculated value of the preserved pension.[8]

Whether through compulsory preservation or transferability, the value to employees of this protection is restricted for three reasons. Most obviously, if inflation exceeds 5%, preserved rights of early leavers will lag behind those who stay.   Second, it takes no account of long run improvements that enable earnings to grow faster than prices.   Finally, final salary schemes particularly favour stayers in careers where real earnings rise over the working life.   The minority OPB report had recommended an 8.5% ceiling instead of 5%, which would have been better, but it was judged to be too destabilising for pension schemes by the majority.   We do not however accept the arguments that full protection against inflation would be 'too costly': this is to admit that the early leaver is being asked to subsidise the benefits of the stayer and therefore also, by extension, the employer. Rather, preservation of rights schould be <u>complete</u> in order to enforce equality of treatment in an area which is closed and confusing to all but the most enquiring eye.   If the overall level of private pension benefits is reduced somewhat then so be it: this is a matter for open negotiation and bargaining between employer and workers.

(d)   General Social Policy:
Fringe benefits policy cannot be consistently separated from other social policy objectives.   Therefore additional implications arise, in particular for the provision of medical health insurance.   Since the current government policy is to foster the private medical sector, it is consistent to encourage the provision of such insurance.   As we explained above we take the opposite view, that private medicine should be discouraged.   We would wish to augment limitations to private medicine generally by constraining its provision by companies, preferably by legally abolishing it.

The Short and the Long Term
The various policies which we advocate in the previous section can be summed up by the propositions that fringes should not be encouraged by tax privileges and that they should be governed by certain controlling legislation in the interests of greater equality, openness and efficiency.

It might nonetheless be argued that, despite accepting the static principles underlying the proposals, the historical fact that fringe benefits are now provided in a big way, combined with the disruption involved in policy changes implies that it would be better to continue with the present haphazard policies of encouragement.   In this section we aim to answer this objection in respect of the two main fringes for which it is commonly made: pensions and company cars.

(i)   Pensions:

Any future policy must take into account the present partnership of
the state and company sectors in pension provision.   From this, it
has generally been presumed for many years by governments of all per-
suasions that occupational pensions are here to stay since to get rid
of them would cause serious disruption in financial markets.   The
funds are seen as a major source of equity capital for industry as
well as of demand for gilts and Treasury Bills.   But like all 'status
quo' arguments, this needs to be justified in terms of expected adjustment costs rather than used as a blanket rejection of change.
The Occupational Pensions Board ruled out, after only the briefest
consideration, the possibility of radical change in the following terms.

> 'Our aim was to establish those changes within the
> context of the present structure which might alle-
> viate the problems of early leavers without dis-
> turbing large areas of the nation's financial and
> economic life.   In deciding to take this course
> we were influenced by the consideration that basic
> structural changes would take a long time to carry
> out and would involve detailed consultation with
> many different interests ...'
> (Occupational Pensions Board, 1981)

These statements do not provide a valid objection to our proposals.[9]
All substantial changes need wide consultation - that is the essence
of democracy.   To reject changes on this ground alone would be to
rule out democratic change anywhere in social life.   Moreover, the
supposed disruption to the financial system is stated but never argued
through;   nor has any evidence been offered to support this fear.

In fact the effect of a switch away from private towards state pensions
may cause little or no disruption in the long run.   Increased payments
to the state, at the expense of reduced contributions to the occupational sector, would alongside the increased tax revenues as exemptions
are removed augment the income of the state.   Other things being
equal, the level of government borrowing would fall.   Hence the reduction in the supply of funds to financial markets would be matched
by a fall in the government broker's demands upon these funds.

The net effect on the markets would depend on changes in the level of
total savings. Evidence suggests that occupational pension savings
do not substitute with other forms of private saving (Green, 1981;
Hemmings and Harvey, 1983);   hence the fall in occupational pension
saving would also mean a fall in total saving.   Meanwhile savings
through an expanding state scheme rise, with an uncertain effect on
other types of saving.   These effects are further complicated by the
increased redistributive effect of the state scheme which, like all
redistributive measures, would tend to raise consumption and lower
saving, since the rich are on average able to save more than the poor.

But if savings fall, other methods may be used to raise or maintain the level should this be the aim of policy - including interest rate adjustments, general demand management and raising the level of the government's own saving.

It would seem strange, therefore, to argue objections on the grounds that financial markets cannot adjust in the long run to changes in the saving rate. However, would the short-run adjustment costs be too great? Or, to put it the other way round, must we assume that they are necessarily so large as to rule out for ever the benefits of a change in pensions policy? We think not. The onus is on those who rule out change on these grounds to show why the costs are likely to be so great. To begin with, our proposals are not to abolish the schemes - just to remove the socially unjust tax privileges and to control them. This would undoubtedly cut the growth of the pension funds and then lead to a decline as employers found it more sensible to pay higher wages and salaries, while employees switched into a beefed-up state scheme. But the funds would not vanish, either over-night or even in the long term. Their withdrawal from the financial markets would thus be gradual - perhaps no faster than their growth has been. If one can believe in the functionality of markets - as surely the supporters of private pension funds must ~ one can presumably also have confidence in their ability to adjust to such changes. There is therefore no valid short-term adjustment cost argument against change, any more than there is a long-term objection.

(ii) Company Cars:
Another 'status quo' objection to our proposals may be the common one that the British motor industry has come to depend on orders from the company fleet car managers, and that any disruption would spell disaster for British firms and jobs. Thus, it is felt, income tax policy should be subordinated to industrial policy in this case.

It would perhaps be unfair to single out the British government for special reprobation in this, its underhand subsidy strategy. Although unique in its support for company cars amongst European governments, other countries also have their concealed subsidies. There may at times be valid arguments for protection, and we do not propose to assess whether they apply here in respect of the British motor industry in the 1980's.

However, it is now unlikely that the current company car policy really is beneficial for the British motor industry. The 'buy British' policy has helped to orientate the industry towards the sorts of cars the companies want: relatively large ones. Meanwhile domestic industry failed to come up with appropriate models for the rising small car markets and increasingly fell behind in the race. The demand for small cars had to be satisfied by imports. This was aided by the private buyer's search for an individualistic image. As the Guardian correspondent remarked (on October 21st, 1981):

117

> One of the best-known quirks of the British
> new car market is that fleet managers buy
> Fords. This assures Ford of a steady
> market, but on the other hand it gives their
> cars the 'company rep' image which makes so
> many private buyers steer clear and opt for
> something foreign.

Thus the long-run dynamic impact of companies' favouring a particular
type of car may be detrimental due to such indirect effects.

Even apart from the question of indirect outcomes, the direct impact
on Brisith industry is less than before, despite the growing company
car industry. By the late 1970s many companies widened the basis of
their policy to buy 'EEC'. Only 47% of companies were for UK based
manufacturers only (Ford, British Leyland, Vauxhall, Talbot) though
others still bought these cars heavily. However 'UK based' does not
nowadays mean 'made in the UK'. Internationalisation of the industry
has meant that, for example, Ford (an American-owned company) imports
many of its cars or car parts from Germany and elsewhere. As a result,
company car imports grew faster than private car imports; by 1983 the
value of net company car imports exceeded that of private cars (Potter
and Cousins, 1983). Even those makers that remain excluded from the
British company car market on ideological grounds, notably Japanese
and Comecon car makers, may not suffer too badly. The margins on
private sales are greater as there is less wheeling and dealing on
price.[10]

We conclude that, if the British motor industry is capable of surviv-
ing at all, it would certainly be able to cope with the removal of tax
exemptions for company cars. There would still be a substantial demand for them, as they would be needed for genuine company business
(which would remain chargeable to the firms' costs). The main objections are likely to come from private users who would lose their
tax privileges, but they will find it hard to defend them validly and
will need to reveal sheer self interest.

The Privatisation of Sick Pay

Our proposals in this chapter have offered suggestions as to how a
fringe benefit policy should be framed, based on certain objectives.
We may also use the latter to evaluate policy changes, as they occur.
The removal of state sickness benefits (SSB) and their substitution by
Statutory Sick Pay (SSP) in 1983 constituted the most substantial recent policy switch concerning the payment of fringe benefits. How
does the new legislation measure up against our principles of equality,
efficiency and openness?

Before April 1983 employees who had paid sufficient National Insurance
contributions, and who were ill, were eligible for SSB after 3 days of
illness, for a period of thirteen weeks, after which it became 'inval-
idity benefit'. The 'waiting' period of 3 days would not apply twice
within any eight week period. SSB was not taxed, and on top of the

basic benefit, dependants' allowances were made, raising it by some 60 to 70%. Under the new scheme, all employees are eligible for SSP, after 3 days illness. The employer continues to pay it for up to eight weeks, reclaiming the payments from the Department of Health and Social Security (DHSS). Waiting periods of 3 days now have to be served for each illness unless successive spells fall within 2 weeks of each other. After eight weeks the state resumes responsibility.

This legislation is an example of how policies on social welfare and on fringe benefits are closely related. Its introduction modifies the terms of private sick leave arrangements, so that the net effect must be judged by examining private and social welfare together. It conforms to the general ideological stance of the Conservative government, which is to transfer activities to the private sector whenever possible. The explicit intentions were two-fold: bringing short-term benefits within the tax net, with the consequent removal of cases of overcompensation for sickness; and making savings on administration costs. On the face of it, these stated intentions are neutral in respect of equality and of openness, and suggest efficiency improvements. Yet during the period of consultation commentators from both sides of industry pointed to features which suggested that in practice the second intention would not be achieved, and that it might well lead to greater inequality.[11]

Let us examine first the issue of whether the change has brought efficiency gains. Under the previous system, SSB was not taxed. Hence, when SSB was paid in addition to employer's pay under an occupational scheme, it could lead to net pay being greater when ill than when fit and working. This 'anomaly' was said to create an incentive for employees not to go to work. Under the new system the anomaly is removed, but it is highly questionable whether it makes a significant impact on work incentives. The amount of 'overpayment' applied only to some, and was not worth very much given the abolition of earnings-related supplements. There is no compelling evidence that sick pay raises absenteeism substantially; as Cunningham (1981) writes, in 1976 industries with lower absence rates tended if anything to have better sick pay coverage. If employers had found the previous system caused unreasonable disincentives, they could always have re-negotiated the terms of their schemes. Clearly, some disincentive to stop sick people returning to work is beneficial for the employer: it inhibits the spread of diseases to the rest of the workforce.

As for savings on administration costs, the government aimed to cut 3,175 jobs at the DHSS, worth some £30 million a year. This, however, has to be compared to the raised administration costs for firms. The government's argument was that since most workers were also covered by an occupational scheme, payment of SSP would not add substantially to private costs. The Select Committee of the House of Commons, when considering the legislation called for such costs to be monitored, but this exercise would be expensive in itself if not impossible. The CBI estimated the extra private administration costs would be over £130 million (Lewis, 1982). Moreover, one effect of the change is that sick pay has entered the bargaining arena, which itself raises negotiating costs for both employers and trade unions. On the other hand Income Data Services (1984) report that the transfer to SSP has been smoother than feared, with less teething problems than might have been expected. But there is no concrete overall information on how much private costs have turned out to be, except to say that they are substantial. It remains dubious as to whether the government's intentions regarding efficiency will be achieved. A final unknown factor is the likelihood that many employees who receive basic SSP only will be forced to claim Supplementary Benefits, thus limiting the possible cost savings at the DHSS.

Turning next to the issue of payment levels and inequality the situation here is also unclear. Under the new system, some households are better off. New workers with no National Insurance contributions record are immediately eligible for SSP, as are workers who pay reduced rate contributions: beforehand, neither could claim SSB. Moreover, for single people on higher incomes the SSP rates are greater than the old SSB rates. However, a larger number of people, married workers and those with dependents, are substantially worse off than before if they have no occupational scheme as well.

For those who do receive this particular 'fringe benefit', the main impact we can be certain about is the introduction of sick pay into the bargaining process. The outcome depends partly on the powers of the negotiating parties, and partly on the type of scheme that previously existed. In 'inclusive' schemes, employers made up the difference between SSB and a certain percentage of pay. In such cases there is little pressure for change since now the employer pays SSP instead but claims it back from the DHSS. In 'exclusive' schemes, the employer paid a certain percentage of pay (or a fixed sum) and the employee claimed SSB in addition. In these cases, it is easy for employers to pay the same percentage as before and claim part of it (as SSP) back from the DHSS. Employees are therefore forced to negotiate a rise in their sick pay just to avoid a cut in their overall income. The Trades Union Congress before the law was implemented advised their members to seek agreements whereby 'the total amount received, after tax and NI deductions, from the employer including SSP should not be any less than the total amount received now from occupational sick pay and NI state benefit combined'.[12] Income Data Services (1984) suggest that forcing unions to consider and negotiate over the introduction of SSP has itself brought greater benefits but it is not clear whether those previously on 'exclusive' schemes have gained or lost overall. Moreover they do not comment on the terms that have been introduced in the non-union sector where it was feared that such workers, often with poor relations with their employer, and with insufficient grasp of the intricacies of the new system, would find their overall sick pay entitlements reduced. We cannot judge, at the time of writing, whether this fear was justified.

In sum, this preliminary assessment suggests that the new system, as far as it is possible to tell, is not fulfilling the government's expectations in saving administration costs, and that it may substantially increase inequality.   It can hardly have been intended that the administration functions would simply be shifted on to the private sector: public expenditure on the DHSS is matched by private expenditure which is reflected in higher unit costs.   The aim was to cut out some duplication of functions, but as we have seen other functions have increased and the new system may well be less efficient.

Conclusion

In this final chapter we have argued that, since fringe benefits have become so important, governments should now aim for a consistent overall strategy with clearly defined objectives.   This proposition reinforces our earlier plea for more information to be collected by those government statistical agents that have the resources, preferably through one of the existing annual exercises such as the Family Expenditure Survey.   This would be necessary to monitor both the positive and the negative effects of any fringe benefit policy.   Even, however, in the absence of such a policy, fringes are now too large to be neglected in the study of labour markets.   We need to know better who (from which income and occupation groups) are gaining pension rights and how much they are worth.   Who are entitled to occupational sick pay on top of Statutory Sick Pay, and what are the terms of the schemes?   Who is driving a company car and how much is it worth? And so on.   Until these things can be accurately monitored every year economic analysis of the British labour market will remain that much impoverished.

For our part, we have formulated our proposals based on the empirical results obtained earlier and on three objectives: equality, openness and efficiency.   In short, certain benefits (such as holidays, sick pay and so on) should be provided equally for all up to minimum levels: they should be regarded as 'rights at work', not as on the 'fringes' of work available only to a lucky section of the workforce.   Meanwhile other benefits should not be encouraged by tax exemptions and where they survive some should be subject to certain controls in order to prevent harmful economic and social effects.

Footnotes

1. In 1979, the Chancellor of the Exchequer stated: 'Perks are an inefficient and often wasteful way of rewarding effort, and unjust. Some perks are taxed in full, others pay no tax on identical benefits. The whole chaos might almost have been designed to set people enviously against each other and so to bring our system into contempt;' (quoted in the Financial Times, 28.4.84).

2. See Green (1981) for empirical estimates.

3. See Potter and Cousins, 1983.

4. See Ch. 2, footnote 4.

5. In response to our earlier pamphlet (Smail, Green and Hadjimatheou, 1984) the Daily Express editorial (20.2.84) said that perks for high paid executives offended our 'misguided zeal for equality' ... but we 'are not honest enough to admit as much'. Naturally we do not accept that an egalitarian approach is misguided, but there was no question there nor is there here of disguising our stance.

6. A similar conclusion is arrived at by Reddin (1983), based on similar principles.

7. Calculated from Government Actuary (1978 and 1981).

8. See DHSS (1984). A further proposed measure is for portable individualised pensions. It is not clear at the time of writing whether this will go further in solving the problems of quitting.

9. To be accurate, the Board's remit was solely concerned with the preservation problem, not with the wider issues of this book.

10. See Woodmansey (1982), p.15.

11. For more detailed discussion of plans and shortcoming, see Income Data Services (1983c) and Lewis, (1982).

12. Quoted in Income Data Studies, (1983).

BIBLIOGRAPHY

Alfred Marks Bureau (1983), Survey of Fringe Benefits for Office Staff, Annual Surveys 1975-1983.

Atkinson, A.B. (1983), The Economics of Inequality, 2nd Edition, Oxford University Press.

Bartel, A.P. (1982), "Wages, Nonwage, Job Characteristics and Labour Mobility", Industrial and Labour Relations Review, July, Vol.35, No.4.

Blackburn, R.M. & Mann, M. (1979), The Working Class in Conflict, Macmillan.

Cunningham, M. (1981), Non-Wage Benefits, Pluto, London.

Curran, M.M. (1981), "Interindustry Variations in Male Turnover", British Journal of Industrial Relations.

C.S.O. (1982), Annual Abstract of Statistics, HMSO, London.

C.S.O. (1977), "A Review of the Effects of Taxes and Benefits on Household Income 1961-1975", Economic Trends, January, HMSO, London.

C.S.O. (1978), "Trends in the Distribution of Income", Economic Trends, May, HMSO, London.

C.S.O. (1980), "The Effects of Taxes and Benefits on Household Income 1978", Economic Trends, January, HMSO, London.

C.S.O. (1983), "Effects of Taxes and Benefits on Household Income", Economic Trends, November, HMSO, London.

Department of Employment (annual), New Earnings Survey, HMSO, London.

Department of Employment (1978), "The Pattern of Pay April 1978, key results of the New Earnings Survey", Employment Gazette, HMSO, London.

Department of Employment (1984), "Earnings and Hours for Manual Workers", Employment Gazette, HMSO, London.

Department of Employment (1978), Labour Cost Surveys.

Department of Health and Social Security (1977), Report on a Survey of Occupational Sick Pay Schemes, HMSO, London.

Department of Health and Social Security (1984), Consultative Document on Improved Transferability, for Early Leavers From Occupational Pension Schemes, mimeo, May.

Doeringer, P.B. & Piore, M. (1971), Internal Labour Markets and Man-power Analysis, Lexington Books.

Dunn, A.T. & Hoffman, P.D.R.B. (1983), "Distribution of Wealth in the United Kingdom, Effect of including Pension Rights and Analysis by Age Groups", Review of Economics and Statistics, No.3, September.

Dusenberry, J. (1949), Income, Saving and the Theory of Consumer Be-haviour, Cambridge, Mass. Harvard University Press.

Feldman, R. & Scheffler, R. (1982), "The Union Impact on Hospital Wages and Fringe Benefits", Industrial and Labour Relations Review.

Feuille, P., Hendricks, E.W. & Kahn, M.L. (1981), "Wage and Nonwage Outcomes in Collective Bargaining: Determinants and Tradeoffs", Journal of Labour Research, Spring.

Freeman, R.B. (1981), "The Effects of Unionism on Fringe Benefits", Industrial and Labour Relations Review, July.

Gordon, D. (1972), Economic Theories of Poverty and Underemployment, D.C. Heath.

Gordon, D.M., Reich, M. & Edwards, R.C. (1982), Segmented Work, divided workers, the Historical Transformation of Labour in the United States, Cambridge University Press.

Government Actuary (1978), Occupational Pension Schemes 1975, HMSO, London.

Government Actuary (1981), Occupational Pension Schemes 1979, HMSO, London.

Green, F.G. (1982a), "Occupational Pension Schemes in British Capital-ism", Cambridge Journal of Economics, No.6.

Green, F.G. (1982b), "Fringe Benefits and the Search for Jobs", Kingston Polytechnic Discussion Papers in Political Economy, No.42.

Green, F.Gl (1981), "The Effect of Occupational Pension Schemes on Savings in the United Kingdom. A Test of the Life-Cycle Hypothesis", Economic Journal, March.

Green, F.G., Hadjimatheou, G. & Smail, R. (1984a), "The Growth and In-equality of Fringe Benefits", Kingston Polytechnic Discussion Papers in Political Economy, No.49.

Green, F.G., Hadjimatheou, G. & Smail, R. (1984b), "Fringe Benefits in British Industry", Kingston Polytechnic Discussion Papers in Political Economy, No.51.

Gustman, A. & Segal, M. (1972), "Wages, Wage Supplements and the Inter-action of Union Bargains in the Construction Industry", Industrial and Labour Relations Review, January.

Hawkesworth, R.I. (1977), "Fringe Benefits in British Industry", British Journal of Industrial Relations, Vol. XV, No.3.

Hay-MSL Ltd. (1976), Analysis of Managerial Remuneration in the United Kingdom and Overseas, Royal Commission on the Distribution of Income and Wealth, Background Paper to Report No.5, HMSO, London.

Hemmings, R. & Harvey, R. (1983), "Occupational Pension Scheme Member-ship and Retirement Saving", Economic Journal, March.

Inbucan Management Consultants (Annual), Survey of Executive Salaries and Fringe Benefits, AIC/Inbucan.

Income Data Services (1983a), Public Sector Bargaining, Study, 303, December.

Income Data Services (1983b), Private Health Insurance, Study, 292, June.

Income Data Services (1983c), Introductory SSP, The Current State of Play, Study 283, February.

Income Data Services (1984), Sick Pay and SSP, Study 316, June.

Inland Revenue Statistics (1983), HMSO, London.

Institute of Directors, (1983), Directors Rewards Part I (1983/4), Institute of Directors and Reward Regional Surveys Ltd., Staffs.

Kalamotousakis, G. (1972), "Statistical Analysis of the determinants of Employee Benefits by type", American Economists, Fall.

Kincaid, J.C. (1973), Poverty and Equality in Britain: A Study of Social Security and Taxation, Harmondsworth, Penguin.

Lawler, E.E. & Levin, E. (1968), "Union, Officers' Perception of Members' Pay Preferences", Industrial and Labour Relations Review, July.

Lawson, T. (1981), "Paternalism and Labour Market Segmentation Theory", in Wilkinson, F. (ed) The Dynamics of Labour Market Segmentation, Academic Press.

Leigh, D.E. (1981), "The Effect of Unionism on Workers' Valuation of Future Pension Benefits", Industrial and Labour Relations Review, July.

Lester, R. (1967), "Benefits as a preferred form of Compensation", Southern Economic Journal.

125

Lewis, R. (1982), "The Privatisation of Sickness Benefit", _Industrial Law Journal_, December.

Lurie, M. (1965), "The Effect of Non-Vested Pension on Mobility: A Study of the Higher Education Industry", _Industrial and Labour Relations Review_, XVIII, January.

Mabry, B. (1972), "The Economics of Fringe Benefits", _Industrial Relations_, February.

Main, B.G.M. (1982), "The Length of a Job in Great Britain", _Economica_, August.

Mars, G. (1983), _Cheats at Work_, Unwin.

Matsukawa (1977), "Differences in the Fringe Benefits among Japanese Industries", _Osaka Economic Papers_, December.

Merrilees, W. (1981), "Interindustry Variations in Job Tenure", _Industrial Relations_, Vol.20, No.2.

Minns, R. (1980), _Pension Funds and British Capitalism_, Heinemann.

Mitchell, R. (1981), "Fringe Benefits and the Costs of Changing Jobs", _National Bureau of Economic Research_, Conference Paper Series, No.96.

Murlis, H. (1974), _Employee Benefits Today_, British Institute of Management Survey Report, No.3.

Murlis, H. (1976), _Business Cars_, British Institute of Management.

Murlis, H. (1978), _Employee Benefits_, British Institute of Management, Survey Report, No.37.

Murlis, H. & Grist, J. (1976), _Towards Single Status_, British Institute of Management, Survey Report, No.30.

Newby, H. (1977), "Paternalism and Capitalism", in Scase, R. (ed), _Industrial Society: Class Cleavage and Control_, Allen and Unwin, London.

Norris, G.M. (1978), "Industrial Paternalism, Capitalism and Local Labour Markets", _Sociology_, Vol.12.

Office of Population and Census Survey, _General Household Survey_, (1976).

Pindyck, R. & Rubinfield, D.C. (1981), _Econometric Models and Economic Forecasts_, McGraw Hill.

Pond, C. (1980), "Tax Expenditure and Fiscal Welfare", in Sandford, C., Pond, C. & Walker, R. (eds), _Taxation and Social Policy_, Heinemann.

Potter, S. (1983), The Scope for Tax Avoidance by the Corporate Provision of Motoring, Working Paper, Faculty of Social Sciences, Open University.

Potter, S. & Cousins, S. (1983), State Subsidies and the Corporate Motorist, Proceedings at Planning and Transport Research and Computation Ltd., 11th Summer Annual Meeting, London, July.

Rao, P. & Miller, R.L. (1971), Applied Econometrics, Belmont (Calif.) Wadsworth Pub. Co.

Reddin, M. (1983), "Pensions, Wealth and the Exclusion of Inequality", in Field, F. (ed), The Wealth Report, 2nd Edition, Routledge & Kegan Paul.

Reid, G.L. & Robertson, D.J. (1965), Fringe Benefits, Labour Costs and Social Security, Allen and Unwin.

Review Body on Top Salaries (1982), (Chairman Lord Plowden), Report No.18 Fifth Report on Top Salaries, cmnd. No.8552, HMSO, London.

Rice, R.G. (1966), "Skill, Earnings and the Growth of Wage Supplements" American Economic Review, May.

Royal Commission on the Distribution of Income and Wealth (1976), (Chairman Lord Diamond), Report No.3, Higher Incomes from Employment, cmnd. No.6383, HMSO, London.

Royal Commission on the Distribution of Income and Wealth (1979), Report No.7, Fourth Report on the Standing Reference, HMSO, London.

Rubery, J. (1978), "Structural Labour Markets Worker Organisation and Low Pay", Cambridge Journal of Economics, March.

Schiller, B.R. & Weiss, R.D. (1979), "The Impact of Pensions on Firm Attachment", Review of Economics and Statistics, August.

Smail, R., Green, F. & Hadjimatheou, G. (1984), Unequal Fringes, Report No.15, Low Pay Unit Publications, February.

Solnick, M. (1978), "Unionism and Fringe Benefits", Industrial Relations, February.

Townsend, P. (1979), Poverty in the United Kingdom, Penguin.

Viscusi, W.K. (1979), Employment Hazards: An Investigation of Market Performance, Harvard University Press.

Ward, S. (1981), Pensions, Pluto Press.

Wilkinson, F. (ed), (1981), The Dynamics of Labour Market Segmentation, Academic Press.

Woodbury, S.A. (1981), "Estimating Preferences for Wage and Nonwage Benefits", <u>National Bureau of Economic Research</u>, Conference Paper, No.102, February.

Woodbury, S.A. (1983), "Substitution, Between Wage and Nonwage Benefits", <u>American Economic</u> Review, March.

Woodmansey, M. (1982), <u>Business Cars</u>, Management Survey Report, No. 53, British Institute of Management.

INDEX

Accommodation linked to job
7,63-65
age of employee 58
Alfred Mark Bureau Survey 53
assistance with childrens
education 24-25
Automobile Association 29

Bartel, A.P. 50
benefits-in-kind 9-10, 24, 80-81
Blackburn, R.M. 50, 51
Braverman, H. 51
British Institute of Management
13, 17, 53
B.U.P.A. 21

company cars 2, 10-11, 19-21, 29,
39, 69-70, 117-118
company shares 24
Confederation of British Industry
(CBI) 119
Cousins, S. 29
creche 112
Cunningham, M. 29, 41, 104, 119.
Curran, M.M. 50

Department of Employment 7, 10,
53
Department of Health and
Social Security 29,119
Doeringer, P.B. 47
Dunn, A.T. 29
Duesenberry, J. 104

Economies of Scale 45
Edwards, R.C. 46, 47
efficiency 110
Employment Protection Act 98
equality 110

Feldman, R. 52
Feuille, P. 52
Freeman, R.B. 46, 49, 51, 52
Fringes:
 definition of 6-7
 demand for 43-46
 distribution of 11,28, 40 55, 83.
 growth of 2-4, 27-28, 119, 103.
 supply of 41-43
 taxation of 2, 40, 43, 112-114.

General Household Survey, 53, 55
Gordon, D.M. 46, 47
Government Actuary Survey 12, 14.
government policies 91-92
Green, F. 29, 41, 43, 89, 92,
116, 122.
Grist, J. 12, 17.

Hadjimatheou, G. 89, 122
harmonisation 114
Harvey, R. 116
Hawkesworth, R.I. 49, 52
Hay, M.S.L. Ltd. 26
Hemmings, R. 116
Hoffman, P.D.R.B. 29
holidays 1, 2, 8-9, 18, 70-71.

Income distribution 6, 21, 22, 25.
income elasticity 45, 49.
Incomes Policies 2, 94-98, 109.
inequality 2, 3, 4, 11, 25-27.
Institute of Directors 30
internal labour markets 41

Kalamotousakis, G. 52
Kincaid, J.C. 110

Labour Cost Survey 7, 50, 53, 74.
Lawler, E.E. 52
Lawson, T. 43, 53, 75
Leigh, D.E. 52
Lester, B. 50, 52
Levin, E. 52
Lewis, R. 122
life assurance 23
Linear Probability Model 55-58, 67.
loans for home purchase and other
purposes 23

Mabry, B. 46, 52
Mann, M. 50, 51
Mars, G. 5
Matsukawa 50
meal benfits 22-23
meal vouchers 7, 71
medical insurance 2, 21-22
Merrilees, W. 50
Miller, R.L. 88
Minns, S.R. 108
Mitchell, R. 50

Murlis, H. 12, 17, 52, 104

National Health Service 4, 109
Newby, H. 43
Norris, G.M. 43

Occupational Pensions Board 116
Okun 47
openness 110

Paternalism 42-43
pensions, occupational 1, 3,
  11-16, 29, 61-63, 68-69, 116-117
pension funds 3
Pindyck 55
Piore, M. 47
Pond, C. 110
Potter, S. 104, 110

Quitting 41-42, 50

Race Relations Act 98
Rao, P. 88
Reich, G.L. 46, 47
Reid, G.L. 49, 50, 51
Review Body on Top Salaries 20,
  26, 30
Rice, R.G. 49, 51, 52
Robertson, D.J. 49, 50, 51
Royal Commission on the Distrib-
  ution of Income and Wealth 21
Rubery, J. 47
Rubinfield, D.C. 55

Scheffler, R. 52
Schiller, B.R. 50
search model 41
secondary labour markets 1, 51
Segal, M. 52
segmented labour markets
Sex Discrimination Act 98
sick pay 1, 3, 8, 16-18, 58-61,
  67-68, 118-121
Smail, R. 89, 122
Social Policy 115
Social Security Pensions Act 98
Solnick, M. 49, 51, 52
subsidised meals 1, 9-10, 71-72
  81-82

Tax policies 92-93
tenure 41, 49-50, 84, 99, 101

Townsend, P. 5, 11,25, 49, 51,
  52, 53, 55, 65, 73
Townsend, Survey 65
trade unions 3, 45-46
tyre worker 51-52, 85, 100

Unemployment 99, 101
union membership 52-53, 86,
  100-101

Viscusi, K. 49, 50, 52
Voluntary Social Welfare Payments 7-8, 77-79

Wages 48-49, 84, 99
Ward, S. 104
Weiss, R.D. 50
Wilkinson, F. 47
Woodbury, S.A. 49, 51
Woodmansey, M. 122

Occasional Papers on Social Administration No 75

Editorial Committee under the Chairmanship of
Professor Brian Abel-Smith
London School of Economics and Political Science

UNEQUAL FRINGES
fringe benefits in the United Kingdom

Related titles in the Occasional Papers series available from the Bedford Square Press

The Poor and the Poorest *B Abel-Smith* and *P Townsend*
French Pensions *T Lynes*
Income Redistribution and the Welfare State *A Webb* and *J Sieve*
The Distribution and Redistribution of Incomes *D Piachaud*
Making Ends Meet *S Kerr*
Unemployment, Social Policy and Poverty in Europe *R Mitton, P Willmott* and *P Willmott*
In Search of the Scrounger *A Deacon*

Other recent titles in the Series:

Unmet Needs and the Delivery of Care *Paul Chapman*
Aids and Adaptations *U Keeble*
Allocating the Home Help Services *N Howell, D Boldy* and *B Smith*
How Many Patients? *J Butler*
Supplementary Benefits and the Consumer *E Briggs* and *A Rees*
Dependency with Dignity *B Wade, L Sawyer* and *J Bell*
Changing Social Policy *C Walker*
Families at the Centre *P Willmott* and *S Mayne*
Cost Containment in Health Care *B Abel-Smith*
Testing the Safety Net *G Beltram*

Forthcoming

Eileen Younghusband: a biography *K Jones*
Lone Mothers, Paid Work and Social Security *J Bradshaw, A Maynard, D Piachaud* and *A Weale*